Fishing Out of Stonington

Voices of the Fishing Families of Stonington, Connecticut

Fishing Out of Stonington

Voices of the Fishing Families of Stonington, Connecticut

Edited by FRED CALABRETTA

Introduction by GLENN S. GORDINIER

Conclusion by JOHN ODIN JENSEN

Mystic Seaport
75 Greenmanville Ave.
P.O. Box 6000
Mystic, CT 06355-0990

Manufactured in the United States of America

Designed by Caroline Rowntree
Printed by Walsworth Publishing Company

Photographs of the Stonington fishermen, pages 36-223, were taken by Mary Anne Stets, Curator of Photography at Mystic Seaport, with the exception of the following. Fred Calabretta, Associate Curator of Collections and Oral Historian at Mystic Seaport, took the photographs on pages 39, 41, 51, 73, 75, 79, 83, 85, 87, 91, 121, 123, 127, 131, 129, 151, 169, 178, 191, 199, 201, 203, and 205. Dennis A. Murphy, Photographer at Mystic Seaport, took the photographs on pages 36, 49, 51, 56, 59, 89, 135, 163, 171, 197, and 207.

The Stonington Fishing Oral History Project and production of this volume were generously supported by grants from the Community Foundation of Southeastern Connecticut

THE COMMUNITY FOUNDATION
of Southeastern Connecticut

Cataloging-in-Publication Data

Fishing out of Stonington : voices of the fishing families of Stonington, Connecticut / edited by Fred Calabretta ; introd. by Glenn S. Gordinier ; conclusion by John Odin Jensen.—Mystic, Conn. : Mystic Seaport, c2004.
p. : ill., ports. ; cm.
Includes bibliographical references.

1. Fishers—Connecticut—Stonington—Interviews. 2. Fisheries—Connecticut—Stonington—History. 3. Oral history. I. Calabretta, Fred, 1950-. II. Gordinier, Glenn S. III. Jensen, John O.

SH222.C8 F57 2004

ISBN 0-939510-94-4

Contents

Preface

This volume provides a glimpse of the Stonington fishing industry. It captures a moment in time: essentially a three-year period from 1993 through 1996. It does not attempt to offer a complete history of Stonington's commercial fishing industry, nor does it include all of the individuals who were associated with the fishing community during the project's active period.

In April of 1993, with the support of the Community Foundation of Southeastern Connecticut, Mystic Seaport established the Stonington Fishing Oral History Project. The primary goal of the project was to collect and preserve a record of the people, activities, and traditions of the Stonington fishing fleet.

From the moment of its inception, the project was designed to utilize oral history methodology as the primary means of documentation. The story of the Stonington fleet would be collected from the fishermen and those close to them, and recorded in their own words. By sharing their experiences and their views of the fishing lifestyle, they would enrich this newly created collection with insight, immediacy, and emotion that would otherwise be unavailable. The scope of the project was clearly defined. The emphasis would be on people, rather than vessels, gear, or fishing technology. Fishermen were the primary target group for oral histories. Additionally, in establishing preliminary lists of interview candidates, efforts were made to include family members, individuals in supporting activities, and others associated with the fishing industry in significant ways. This would help establish the story of the fishermen in a broader context.

Chronologically, the project was intended to document the people of the current fleet—those individuals with a direct connection to the Stonington fishing industry today. Project documentation would provide an insightful snapshot of an industry in transition. The Stonington fishing fleet is strongly rooted in tradition. For that reason, and to provide additional context for the contemporary industry, an effort was also made to document the earlier twentieth-century history of the fleet. Ultimately, recollections dating back as early as the 1920s were obtained.

Stonington Harbor, and more specifically the Stonington Town Dock, provided the geographical center for the study. Interviews were conducted with a few individuals whose experience was based substantially outside of Stonington. These individuals were included because their experiences were relevant to the study, often on multiple levels.

Project staff also made a decision to incorporate photography as an additional means of documentation that would complement the oral histories. This would add a significant visual component to the project. Black-and-white photography was the primary medium employed, and was chosen primarily for its documentary and aesthetic value. Some color photographs were also taken, and some videotape footage was recorded.

The fishing community was generally extremely supportive of the project. Arthur Medeiros, president of the regional fishermen's association, was the first point of contact. He provided a very useful overview of the Stonington fleet, as well as important and ongoing support and cooperation. More than 30 individuals provided oral history interviews. A number of additional people, while not interviewed for the project, supported the effort in other ways. They were cooperative during photographic sessions, answered questions, and participated in unrecorded but extremely helpful conversations.

A few individuals choose not to participate in the project. Some were hesitant to take the time to be involved, a decision that is certainly understandable considering the long hours they devote to their work. Others were reluctant to be interviewed or photographed based on their feelings that fishermen had often been misquoted or otherwise misrepresented by the media. They were wary of any effort to capture or represent their story.

Overall, the project achieved its goals and met with considerable success. During a three-year period from 1993 through 1995, a total of 35 interviews were conducted, resulting in more than 40 hours of recorded sound and over 800 pages of transcripts. These materials now form part of the Oral History Collection in the G.W. Blunt White Library at Mystic Seaport. Additionally, more than 1,200 photographs were taken, mostly in black and white, and these are now housed in the Mystic Seaport Photo Archives. The initial success of the project encouraged the continued support of the Community Foundation of Southeastern Connecticut, which generously provided funding for three consecutive years.

An exhibition based upon the project was created, and was on view for six months at Mystic Seaport. This exhibit consisted of printed quotations from the oral history interviews, an audio program comprised of clips from interview recordings, 40 enlargements of project photographs, and accompanying text. The exhibition was well received. At the request of the fishing community, a slightly smaller version of the exhibition has been presented at the Town Dock during the annual Blessing of the Fleet.

Because of limitations of time and budget constraints, the demands of other Mystic Seaport projects and activities, and the busy schedules of the fishermen and lobstermen, the project was not fully comprehensive. It is hoped that the individuals or families receiving only brief mention in this volume, and those perhaps not mentioned at all, will understand the goals of the project and will appreciate what we have tried to accomplish. We also hope they will realize, although their names may not appear in print, that this is their story too. It is the story of their fleet, their industry, and, most importantly, their fishing community. We believe the experiences and emotions of the individuals represented in this volume provide a common thread that connects all the men and woman of Stonington's fishing community, past and present.

The success of the Stonington Fishing Oral History Project, and the creation of this volume, were made possible by the outstanding cooperation and support of the fishing community. We are indebted to the fishermen and their families for sharing their time, stories, and experiences. Among the many individuals who participated in the project, Arthur Medeiros, Ann Rita, and John Rita deserve special thanks. Their friendship, assistance, and encouragement for the past 10 years is greatly appreciated.

Mystic Seaport is grateful to the Community Foundation of Southeastern Connecticut for its generous support. Beginning in 1993, the Foundation provided funding for three consecutive years to help offset project costs, and then awarded an additional grant in 2004 to help underwrite the publication of this book. We value the Foundation's ongoing commitment to this project, and its role in helping the Museum record, preserve, and present this important community story.

This book has been greatly enriched by the contributions of Glenn Gordinier and John Jensen, and by the editorial skills of Andy German. All three share a strong interest in the commercial fishing industry and a deep respect for fishermen and their families. Thanks also to designer Caroline Rowntree.

Two Mystic Seaport staff members deserve extensive credit and thanks for their significant contributions to the Stonington Fishing Oral History Project. Mary Anne Stets, Curator of Photography and Director of Intellectual Property, contributed her wonderful photographic skills and took the majority of the photographs illustrating this book. Glenn S. Gordinier, Ph.D., Robert G. Albion Historian and Co-Director of the Munson Institute at Mystic Seaport, conducted a number of the oral history interviews. Both Glenn and Mary Anne were actively involved in the organization and planning of the project. Mystic Seaport staff members Claire Calabretta, Marie Coste, Sarah Fisher, and Dennis Murphy also made important contributions to the project. I would also like to express my gratitude to my past and present supervisors at Mystic Seaport, Paul O'Pecko and Bill Peterson, for their support of my work on the project.

The following individuals and organizations contributed to the Stonington Fishing Oral History Project by providing interviews, participating in photography sessions, or giving other support or assistance: Walter Allyn, James Allyn, David Angrisani, Albert Banks, Patricia Banks, Richard Bardwell, Carolyn Battista, Ernest Beckwith, Robert Berg, Doris Berg, George Berg, Paul Bergel, Peter Bissette, Bill Bomster Sr., Bill Bomster Jr., Joe Bomster, Mike Bomster, Tom Brelsford, Michael Brennan, Wayne Cale, Alan Chaplaski, Mike Daniels, Rev. Edward J. Davis, John DeBragga, Betty Fellows, Charles Fellows, Lester Gay, Rev. Philip Geogan, John Ghiorse, Arthur Griffin, John Grimshaw, Mike Grimshaw, Robert Guzzo, James Henry, Phil Henry, Frank Keane, Joe Kessler, Rev. William Loftus, Alfred Maderia Sr., Alfred Maderia Jr., Andrew Maderia, Manny Maderia, Richie Maderia, Henry Maxwell, George McCagg, Don McPherson, Jim McPherson, Arthur Medeiros, Jeff Medeiros, Michael Medeiros, Tim Medeiros, Donald Mercer, Jeff Mills, Bill Morrison, Chet Murray, Mike Pont, Paul Previty, Bishop Daniel P. Reilly, Joseph Rendeiro, Robert Rinaldi, Ann Rita, John Rita, Kenny Santos, Sea-Rich Seafoods, Mark Scott, Manny Soares, Blanche Stillman, Robert Stillman Sr., Stonington Fillet Company, Stonington Historical Society, Ziggy Suminski, Mary Thacher, Jay Tillinghast, Phil Torres, Vivian Volovar, Margaret White, Nathan Williams, Mike Winters, Joe Wojtas, and Edward York.

FRED CALABRETTA
Associate Curator & Oral Historian

Individuals Quoted in this Work

Jim Allyn was a successful fisherman and captain of an offshore boat that worked as a dragger and scalloper. He died in 2002 at the age of 43, and is survived by his wife and two children. His father and brother continue to be actively involved in fishing.

Walter Allyn is a veteran of the local waterfront with extensive fishing and boatbuilding experience. He and his son Dave presently own a total of four offshore boats. Walter Allyn is also actively involved with the Southern New England Fishermen's and Lobstermen's Association.

Al and Patty Banks attend the Blessing of the Fleet every summer. It has special meaning to them as a time to remember their son Arthur, who was lost when the Stonington-based offshore lobster boat Heidi Marie sank in 1989.

Dick Bardwell has been the dockmaster in Stonington for many of years. Although he is originally from the Midwest, he has more than 30 years of experience in the commercial fishing industry.

When **Doris Berg** married her husband **George** in 1928, he was already a fisherman. George Berg began working as a commercial fisherman about 1926, and worked out of Stonington for more than 40 years. The couple's two sons followed their father into the fishing trade. **Robert Berg** began fishing with his father about 1950 and worked for many years locally as a commercial fisherman.

At the time he was interviewed in 1994, **Tom Brelsford** was a conservation officer for the State of Connecticut's Department of Environmental Protection. His responsibilities included enforcement of the state's commercial fisheries regulations.

Charlie Fellows began fishing out of Stonington in the 1940s. He and his wife **Betty** were married in 1951. Charlie sold his boat several years ago and retired, and the couple now spends winters in Florida.

Arthur Griffin was born in 1914. Although not from the local area, he worked for a time as a commercial fisherman out of Stonington in the early 1930s.

Mike Grimshaw began lobstering full-time in the 1970s, and he runs one of the largest lobstering operations in the area, with two boats and more than 3,000 pots. He is related to the DeBragga and Roderick families, both with an extensive history of involvement in the Stonington fishing community. Mike is also one of the committee members for the Blessing of the Fleet.

Jim Henry, who turned 91 in 2004, is one of the oldest surviving Stonington fishermen. He began fishing on Stonington draggers in the early 1930s, made many trips as captain, and eventually owned his own boat for a number of years. In the 1960s he switched to lobstering, which he continued for about 20 additional years.

Frank Keane moved to Stonington with his parents in 1913, and he eventually operated a local store for more than 50 years. His brother-in-law was a fisherman, and Frank has always been an interested observer of commercial fishing and community life in Stonington Borough.

Al Maderia grew up in a family with a strong fishing heritage, and is owner and captain of the Stonington dragger Serena. He has grown increasingly frustrated with catch restrictions and other regulations in recent years, and is considering selling his boat.

Manny Maderia grew up in a large Portuguese family, and all of his 10 brothers spent time as fishermen and lobstermen. He worked for years as a commercial fisherman and lobsterman. He is one of few veteran fishermen still living in Stonington borough. At he age of 85, he remains very active, stringing bait and working with his son Richie, also a lobsterman.

Richie Maderia followed his father Manny's path as a lobsterman. He fished as many as 3,000 pots for a number of years, but has since scaled back his lobstering. He is now following another tradition established by his father, operating an active lobster business while also working at Electric Boat Shipyard in Groton. Richie's sons often spend time lobstering with their father.

Arthur Medeiros began fishing in the 1940s and, by the time he retired in 1994, both he and his boat, the *Rosemary R.*, had become fixtures on the Stonington waterfront. Although he no longer goes out fishing, he owns the dragger *Seafarer*, which is operated by his friend John Rita. Arthur remains actively associated with the fishing community, serving as president of the Southern New England Fishermen's and Lobstermen's Association and chairman of the Blessing of the Fleet committee. He has held both positions for more than 20 years.

The son of fisherman Arthur Medeiros, **Michael Medeiros** fished with his father for six months following his graduation from college in 1993. Although he found the experience to be very rewarding, he chose to pursue other interests and is presently working for a company in Texas. He returns with his own family to Stonington every summer to attend the Blessing of the Fleet.

Tim Medeiros comes from a family tradition of fishing, and is the long-time owner and captain of a Stonington dragger. He, his mother, and other family members operate a very successful food concession during the Blessing of the Fleet, with all of the proceeds used to support the next year's event. Drawing upon their food-service experience, in 2002, Tim and his family opened Captain Tim's, a restaurant in Pawcatuck, Connecticut, specializing in seafood prepared in traditional Portuguese style.

Joe Rendeiro was born in Portugal, the son of a fisherman, and he first went fishing with his father at the age of 16. He and his brother Gino were captains of offshore draggers working out of Stonington for many years. Joe retired in 2001 after more than 50 years of fishing, but he remains an active advocate for fishermen.

John and Ann Rita were childhood neighbors and members of Stonington fishing families. John eagerly went fishing with his father as a boy, and has been a commercial fisherman for more than 30 years. He is presently captain of the dragger Seafarer. Ann's father, Manny Mederia, worked as a fisherman and lobsterman, her brother is a lobsterman, and her sister is married to a fishermen. Ann works as the bookkeeper for the Town Dock, and both she and John are actively involved in the organization and management of the Blessing of the Fleet.

Manny Soares is owner and captain of the dragger Stephanie Bryan, which works as both an inshore boat going out daily and an offshore "trip" boat, depending on the season. He first went fishing as a young boy, and learned from his father and members of the Roderick family.

Phil Torres is a Pennsylvania native who first became associated with the Stonington fishing industry about 1987. When he was interviewed in 1994, he was first mate of a boat owned by Walter Allyn and his sons. His skills and experience have helped him to achieve his goal of becoming a captain. He now runs one of the Walter Allyn's boats, which works offshore as a scalloper and dragger.

Ever Changing, Ever Constant:

Stonington Borough and Its Commercial Fishing Fleet

The Borough of Stonington, in the first decade of the twenty-first century is, as one scholar recently noted, "the result of tensions–geographical, cultural, and economic," which over the years has "survived to coexist comfortably and serve new purposes and constituencies." Predestined by nature to be a small, compact community whose character would always be tied to the sea, the Borough has changed little physically over the years, but has changed greatly in its identity.[1] Yet, through the centuries, one element of the village's character has always been present, and that element is its fishing community.

The small, peninsular village of Stonington Borough covers approximately 170 acres of the 25,222 acres that make up the larger town of Stonington. It juts into the western North Atlantic as the most southeastern feature of the state of Connecticut. Long Point, as it was known, was not populated by Europeans until a century after the first settlers established the town of Stonington with their farming homesteads located further inland. Not until the early 1750s did Englishmen build homes on the point called Wadawanuck by the Native Americans. Yet, almost immediately fishing became an important activity among those in the waterside village. The Borough has been a political subdivision of the town since 1801.[2]

By the time of the American Revolution, approximately 500 people lived on Long Point, and they made their living by whaling and codfishing. It is quite likely that at that early date cod was much more vital to the town's survival than the occasional "whale fish." By 1795 it was reported that Stonington was home port to a small number of near-shore codfishermen, as well as a handful of other vessels that fished the Grand Banks, cured their fish on the coast of Newfoundland, and delivered their season's catch in Boston. In addition, blackfish, bass, and crab, being in great abundance locally, occupied a considerable number of small craft. Their catch was maintained in ponds along the shore and then delivered to the New York City market.
Throughout this period, beginning in 1796, the federal government actively supported the codfishing industry. A bounty, based on the tonnage of each vessel was offered to all codfishermen who were active for at least four months a year. This involvement by the government in fishery management lasted for 70 years.[3]

It is worth noting that during the earliest of those years the fishing vessels of southeastern Connecticut were gaining a reputation, both locally and in distant waters, for their qualities as seaboats and as fishing platforms. During the first decade of the nineteenth century, some of these vessels ranged as far south as the Carolinas and Georgia. Then, sailing their sloops (single-masted vessels) even further south, men from Mystic and Stonington were among the earliest settlers of Key West. The fishing vessels they sailed were known as "wet-well smacks" because they included a watertight compartment in their hold that allowed sea water to flush through to keep the catch alive.[4]

A decade later, during the years immediately following the War of 1812, Stonington was reported to have a fleet of 10 to 15 vessels that landed nearly 800,000 pounds of salt cod and 1,000 barrels of cod. Shortly thereafter, in the early 1820s, New York City's Fulton Fish Market was created to serve the demand for fish in the burgeoning city more efficiently. Fishermen from Stonington Borough and Mystic were directly involved in the opening of that largest of fish emporiums. Stonington men and fishing firms continued to have stalls in the Fulton Fish Market over 120 years later.[5]

Stonington's maritime identity during the first half of the 1800s was most directly connected to the whaling and sealing industries. Stonington vessels ranged the world's oceans in search of the oil and baleen of the leviathan, the pelts of seal, and the oil of sea elephants. The village readily assumed the look of a prosperous seaport, as vessels came from and went to distant, exotic places, and the mansions of the shipowners arose on Main Street. In 1839, Stonington residents were known for their "commercial enterprise," yet, it is worth noting as well that the prosaic finfisheries were still an important element of the local economy with "large capitals employed in the whale, seal, and cod fisheries." In that year, the Borough was reported to have 1,200 residents. It was also noted, with some prescience perhaps, that "many strangers visited in summer months to enjoy the marine air and delightful scenery."[6]

The other major activity in the Borough through much of the 1800s was that of the "night boats" of the Stonington Line. This operation, connecting steamboats and steam trains, was one of the most important transport links between New York and Boston. The steamers of the Stonington Line would leave lower Manhattan late each day, travel down the protected waters of Long Island Sound to the Borough through the hours of dark, and link with the railhead at the wharf in Stonington. The twice-daily arrival and departure of these modern conveyances enlivened the village and energized its economy from 1837 to 1904. A large hotel, The Wadawanuck House, was alive with people who were visiting or moving through the little community on a regular basis.[7] These travelers are likely to have enjoyed the products of the Stonington fishing smacks and lobster boats, even while the steamboats they rode carried a portion of the local catch to Fulton Fish Market.

By the early 1860s, whaleships no longer departed Stonington, bound for the South Atlantic or the Pacific. That phase of the Borough's history ended at the time of the Civil War, yet her fishermen continued to set out in search of their more prosaic prey. In 1880, 42 men were reported to have landed over 2,000,000 pounds of menhaden and other fish in Stonington. It appears that most of the fishermen at this time were involved in small-boat fishing as only two vessels of 55 tons were engaged in catching food fish, while there was just a single Stonington menhaden steamer. According to reports, a number of these small-boat fishermen made use of the gillnets, fyke nets, and other apparatus that took a small quantity of fish annually. Stonington lobstermen fished local waters between April and November to serve the local market, but they reported the daily catch was only about 50 pounds per man, whereas it had been as much as 200 pounds per man in the 1860s. They earned about $1.50 per day, which was equivalent to the daily wage of a semiskilled laborer ashore. It is clear that in 1880, although men were still fishing out of Stonington and there was a fish market at the Union Wharf store, the trade in the village was at a low ebb. At that time, more men were involved in fishing and lobstering in neighboring towns than in the Borough.[8] Perhaps this drop off was linked to the end of the government codfishing bounty in 1866.

Stonington's fortunes as a fishing community improved, however, as, by 1893, 47 vessels worked out of Stonington employing 261 men. The additional men were employed in larger vessels and they ranged over grounds that would be familiar to Stonington fishermen a century later.

Small crews put out from the Borough in sloops usually not exceeding 30 feet in length. These smacks primarily fished for cod and haddock with handlines in Block Island Sound. Total landings in Stonington in 1893 exceeded 20,000,000 pounds. It is likely that the largest portion of the catch that landed in Stonington continued to be shipped to the New York market aboard steamboats of the Stonington Line. Ellery Thompson reported that some years later the Stonington steamboats took fish to Fulton Market and that "the service attracted many schooners and smacks to the port because of the ease with which fish could be shipped into New York City."[9]

Fishing smacks lie at the dock in this postcard photograph, ca. 1905.
Mystic Seaport 1989.69.9

During the decades following the Civil War, a new fishing technique was brought to the United States. "Beam Trawling" entailed dragging a net across the fishing grounds as opposed to fishing with baited hooks, and a handful of fishermen on the East and West Coasts experimented with the system. By 1895, this dragging technique was being practiced in New England waters with finfish being harvested much as oysters were dredged, using sloops that relied on wind and tide to propel the vessel and its net across the fishing grounds. Over the next decade, fishermen in the vicinity of Cape Cod met with mixed but growing success with the sail-powered dragging.[10] Greater changes were soon to come.

In 1905 and 1906, the use of internal combustion engines revolutionized the dragging business, as small, eight- and ten-horsepower engines allowed the fishermen to run their nets back and forth over the fishing grounds, even against the wind and tide. The use of larger engines and vessels of increasing size evolved over the next two decades as dragging gained in popularity. Not surprisingly, Stonington's fishermen were quick to profit from this new opportunity. Lobstermen also benefited greatly by the increased mobility

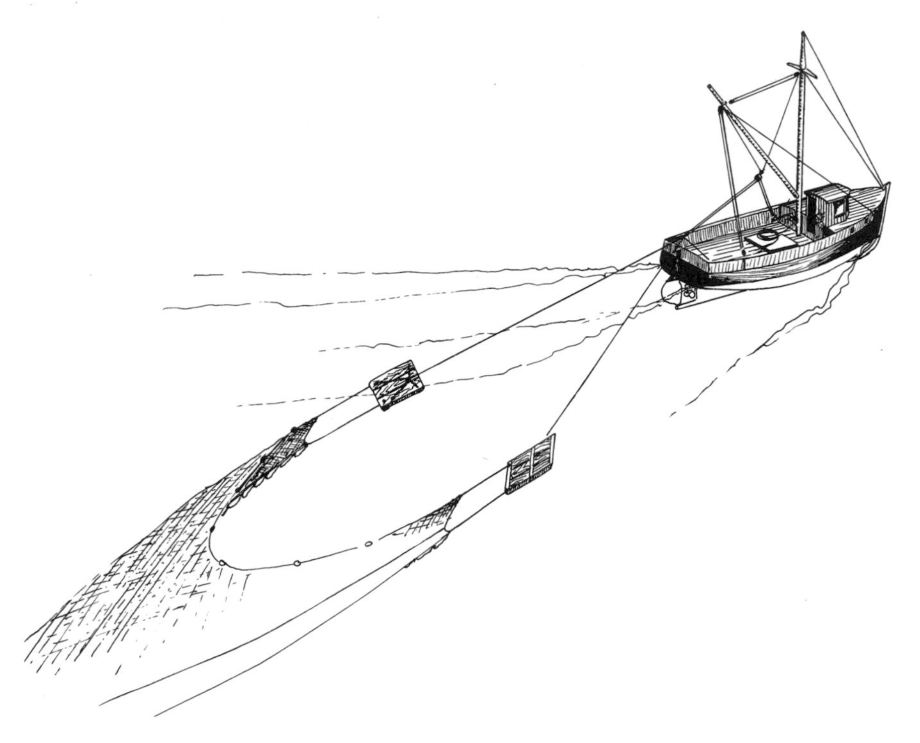

This sketch by Walter Ansel shows the towing arrangement for an otter trawl used by the *Florence* and other western-rig draggers.

offered by using power boats. Lobstering was a slack-tide fishery, and being able to motor to the lobster grounds in spite of wind and weather was a great advantage.[11]

Coincidentally, the completion of the rail line along the New York and New England shore finally caught up with the steamboats of the Stonington Line. In 1904, that venerable connection between water and rail ceased its operations as the railroad bridged the deep Thames River at New London. This engineering accomplishment finally completed the shoreline rail link between New York and Boston. The traffic generated by the steamboats had helped define the cycle of life in Stonington Borough for nearly 80 years. With its demise, the once bustling transportation center slipped into an era of quietude, broken only by the whistles of the two local mills and the regular chug of fishermen's engines on the harbor. The village had evolved once again, but the fishermen and their families carried on even as they too experienced a change in their methods and routines.

Around 1909, Captain Elisha Clark brought a new style of dragging to Stonington from the eastern end of Long Island. Known as otter trawling, this technique was copied by Captain Frank Thompson and other aspiring fishermen.[12] The otter trawl is still used by Stonington fisherman today, just as it is used by powered vessels large and small around the globe. The net of the otter trawl is towed behind the fishing vessel, with its mouth held wide, not by a long beam but by the outward thrust of its two doors, or otter boards, which are on bridles forward of the net. The arrival of the otter trawl in Stonington early in the 1900s altered the lives of the fishermen in a number of ways. More fish were to be harvested, and thus more profit was to be made. In addition, this new technology led the men to buy larger vessels, with more powerful engines with which they could range farther and work more distant fishing grounds in a short span of time.

With their pilothouses located forward, and a broad working deck aft, the Connecticut-built trawlers towed their nets from the stern as opposed to the alternative design that towed abeam. The "eastern rig," which was popular on the Massachusetts coast, combined elements of the big British-style steam trawlers that dragged offshore and the traditional fishing schooner, with its working deck forward and its helm aft. The Connecticut vessels, had been built "up west" relative to the location of the Bay State, and were therefore known as "western rig." Having the pilothouse forward offered the western-rig vessels a number of advantages, including more maneuverability with the towing cables going over the stern. These vessels also gave the helmsman better visibility than those steering from a pilothouse near the stern. This greater visibility was particularly important in the areas Stonington's men worked, where the bottom was often cluttered with rocks or wrecks that would shred fishing gear. These invisible hazards were only avoided by learning their locations through hard earned experience and then identifying those sites by shoreside range markers, which one needed to see without visual obstructions. The western rig also offered the crew working on deck a bit of shelter in the lee of the pilothouse, while the skipper at the helm had ready access to the engine room or foc's'le located directly below.[13]

One effect of the use of larger vessels was a shift in the location of Stonington's fishing activity. Before the otter trawl brought about larger fishing boats, much of the community's fishing activity was centered on the east side of the Borough, at Clay's Dock on Hancox Street. Captain Manuel Clay supported shoreside fisheries such as lobstering, longline trawling, haul seining, and "barrel traps" (a wall of net supported by floating barrels set perpendicular to the shore, which guided migrating fish into a pound (trap) section from which they would be hauled). These fisheries could be carried out from open boats and dories that needed little in the way of deep-water anchorage and access to shore. When the dragger technology demanded larger vessels, the focus of the Borough's fishing industry shifted to the deeper Stonington Harbor on the west side of the village, and Clay's "Little Fulton Fish Market" lost its position as the center for the community's fishing activity.[14]

Several locations in Stonington Harbor vied for the attention of the Borough's fishermen. One of the most important fishing docks on the west side of the village was run by the Bindloss family. Opened by William Bindloss when he took over the failed Samuel Z. Cheseborough Fishing and Trading Corporation, the Bindloss Marine Station would service Stonington fishermen until the late 1960s. The station was located at what had been the old Pendleton Wharf, just north of the large factory operated by Atwood Machine. For many years the dock was managed by John B. Bindloss, son of the original owner. At the time of this printing the site is principally occupied by Skipper's Dock Restaurant.

For a time a small number of fishermen used the lee of a pair of old Long Island Sound steamboats for protection when they tied up. The *Puritan* and *Pilgrim*, measuring 403 and 372 feet respectively, had sped up and down Long Island Sound carrying cargoes and passengers since the early 1880s. In 1914, the hulking old queens of the Sound were moored at the old Railroad Wharf, and a handful of small draggers, handliners, and lobster boats could be found riding quietly in their shadow. A decade later, Nat Avery operated a fishing dock from the old wharf, and for a number of years

The 40-foot western-rig dragger *Florence* lies at the Steamboat Wharf in this 1926 photograph. Courtesy Howard Shaw

Avery's operation was a very active fish-packing station.[15]

Also in 1914, the Franklin G. Post shipyard opened in neighboring Mystic, Connecticut. Originally located on the western (Groton) side of the Mystic River, the yard expanded and moved to the east (Stonington) side of the estuary in 1923. The Post yard was located just downriver from the Cottrell lumber yard, which was adjacent to the highway drawbridge. With an international reputation for yachts, Post also built cargo and fishing vessels, including a number that fished out of Stonington. Among those was the 40-foot *Florence*, launched in 1926. This historic vessel is currently preserved at Mystic Seaport, a half mile north of her birthplace. A fascinating piece of local maritime history, she is a direct link to the Stonington fishermen of the 1920s as she was fished out of the Borough by Captains Morris Thompson and Howard Shaw.[16]

The introduction of internal combustion engines revolutionized America's alongshore fisheries during the first decade of the 1900s. The sound of the "one-lungers" banging their way down the harbor in the light of dawn became common in ports throughout the country, and so it was in Stonington. The most popular engine for these small working boats was the Lathrop two-cycle "make-and-break," which was produced in the company's shop on Holmes Street in Mystic. Founded in 1897, the Lathrop Engine Company refined and perfected internal combustion engines for marine use, most particularly for commercial and fishing applications.[17] A century later, the company's low, white clapboard building still stands on the waterfront, a quarter mile south of Mystic Seaport on the Mystic River.

By the 1920s the dragging technology had served to boost the economy of New England's fishing communities. A case in point was the old whaling port of Nantucket, which came to have a fleet of over fifty 45- to 50-foot draggers. Just as that distant island had found its first fortunes in the whales that migrated past its shores, so did it have a boom in the newly popular flounder fishery that had resulted from the adoption of the beam trawl and otter trawl. For Nantucket fishermen, ready access to the habitat of the flatfish was made possible by the introduction of internal combustion, and the island economy soon benefited. The whaling port of Stonington also prospered as its fishermen invested in Lathrop engines of increasing size, otter trawls, and larger vessels (some with diesel engines) that could work the productive grounds in the neighborhood of Block Island.[18]

The use of increasingly more powerful vessels and more productive gear like the otter trawl enabled the fishermen of Stonington to fish with greater success. Other challenges to their profitability were still an everyday part of their existence, however. Fluctuating prices at the dock, the dangers of the fishery, and shoreside expenses were threats to profitability that the men determined to face cooperatively.

In December of 1931, in the depths of the Great Depression, 125 fishermen met in Mystic, Connecticut, to create their own association. The

Western-rig draggers fill the dock in this photograph, ca. 1935.
Mystic Seaport 1994.121.1

Southern New England Fishermen's Association Inc. was formed under the able leadership of Captain John Smith, master of the *Russel S.* Looking to meet both short-term and long-term challenges, the organization immediately set out to establish an extensive membership whose dues would support the association's goals. Those goals included "the promotion of the fishing industry; to safeguard and save the industry from any unreasonable legislation and to insist upon the right of free and untrammeled commerce, both intra- and inter-state, and such other objects as shall be for the improvement and protection of the fishing industry." With the motto of "All For one and One For All," and a logo consisting of a triangle embracing the words "Harmony, Equality,

Courtesy Arthur Medeiros

Justice" surrounding an oil-skinned fisherman astride a large fish, the unity of the group was made clear. Over the next few years, the organization lobbied in Hartford and Washington, sent delegates to industry meetings in New York and elsewhere, and met with similar organizations. The leadership also addressed the challenge of taxes on the fishing industry and increased navigational safety. In those Depression years, the membership also voted to offer financial support to fishermen who had fallen on hard times. In addition, they developed a group insurance plan with desirable rates for fishing boat coverage. Governmental limitations on fishing were also on the agenda of the association, even in the 1930s. Although the name of the organization has been changed to the Southern New England Fishermen's and Lobstermen's Association, the organization, and its leadership, has continued to work on behalf of its members and the industry since that time. It remains a vital part of that community today.[19]

An early refinement of the Fishermen's Association bears witness to an ongoing reality in the Stonington fishing story. That reality is the vital role played by women in supporting their families, their husbands, and in turn the industry itself. At an association meeting in May of 1934, a motion was made and seconded to form a Women's Auxiliary to the Southern New England Fishermen's Association. The women's organization would, from its inception, be independent of the men's association. This seems most fitting, as the wives and mothers of the Stonington fishing fleet had earned their salt for generations, and, for generations to follow, anyone connected to the fleet understood the vital role these women played in the way of life. As the men put to sea, the women raised the children, maintained a secure home, dealt with shoreside crises, often managed the family economy, and supported their men in a choice of work that had such great impact on themselves. It is a commonplace among the people of this community that the hard work and commitment of these women has always been vital to the success of the fleet.[20]

It is important to note, as well, that the Southern New England Fishermen's Association was actually formed partly in response to an immediate threat to the welfare of the local fishing fleet. The fishermen of Stonington, and other nearby communities, organized in order to counter the threat of increased transport costs for taking their product to the Fulton Fish Market. This incident speaks not only of the ethos of that period, and the resolve of the region's fishermen, but also to the their ongoing dependence on that vital urban market. In November of 1931, "Parties"—as they were described—who were connected to the transport of fish to New York had announced a 25-cent-per-barrel increase in the cost of trucking local fish to the city. Captain Smith determined that this extortion would not stand, and after it appeared that the state would not involve itself, the Southern New England Fishermen's Association was formed. The leadership then hatched a plot that would force the extortion issue. The fishermen would send one truck to New York City loaded with local product. That truck would be followed by a second filled with armed fishermen who would give the transport racketeers "a taste of their own medicine" if there was "any tough stuff." A subsequent meeting between Smith and the state attorney general secured an alternate escort. Ultimately, state troopers from both Connecticut and New York were used to insure safe passage of the local fish to the Fulton marketplace. Smith later confronted gangsters in a Fulton Market fish stall over additional attempts at extortion. His courage and organizational skills earned the gratitude and respect of the region's fishing community for years to come.[21]

As difficult as making a living in commercial fishing was during the Great Depression, by 1938 there were still 52 vessels in the Stonington fleet. Then, utter disaster befell the fleet in one horrifying afternoon, when the hurricane of September 21 devastated the region, the Borough, and the fishing boats themselves. Among those destroyed by that epic storm were Alfred Rubello's *Mary*, Harold McLaughlin's *Marise*, John Smith's *Russel S.*, John Pont's *Pal*, Walter Schroeder's *Ruth*, and George Grogan's *Louise*. These vessels, and their sisters, were driven up on docks or pilings and stove, or broke free of their moorings and raced helter-skelter to leeward up Stonington Harbor, where they were driven ashore. Nearly all were completely destroyed or damaged beyond repair. The *Ruth*, for instance, ended up on the railroad tracks near the abandoned cars of the Bostonian, a passenger train that had been caught in the storm as well. A few vessels could be repaired, including George Berg's *Lindy* and Ellery Thompson's *Eleanor*. Thompson had been lucky when the *Eleanor* fetched up in the tennis courts of the Wadawanuck Club at the head of the harbor. The storm also destroyed the Stonington Boat Works, which Henry R. Palmer had started only six months earlier just south of the old Steamboat Wharf.[22]

The Stonington Boat Works ultimately prospered, however, in part because so much work was to be had repairing or replacing the home fleet. A few years later, the Second World War resulted in rapid growth of Stonington's fishing activity. The booming wartime market and support by the federal government allowed the fleet to expand to 60 vessels, with another 40 departing from the nearby Mystic and Thames Rivers. Many of Stonington's new draggers were built by Palmer's boat works. The first of them, the *Carl J.* worked for many decades, surviving groundings, fire, and even a dockside explosion.[23]

Another operation that expanded during the war was the Bindloss

A crowd at the Bindloss Dock, ca. 1935. Mystic Seaport 1993.17.469

In this 1945 photograph of Bindloss's Dock, Manuel Maderia's 40-foot dragger *Lindy*, built in Stonington in 1927 and powered by an 80-horsepower oil engine, lies at the end of the pier.
Gordon Sweet photograph.
Mystic Seaport 1989.108.30

Marine Station, located at the old Pendelton and coal docks. With the growing demand for fish to aid in the war effort, Bindloss opened a fish fillet plant in 1944. Filleting—the process of cutting the flesh from the bones of landed fish—had proved to be a popular marketing tool during the 1920s as it made cooking fish much more convenient. With no bones and little waste, filleted fish seemed ideal for use by the military. Although the peacetime slowdown resulted in the filleting operation closing six years later, Bindloss's Dock remained a center of commercial fishing and its culture for years to come.[24] Many of the Borough's draggers and lobster boats tied up there, obtained their fuel and ice from Bindloss, and later off-loaded their catch there.

In the 1950s two facilities offered off-loading, packing, and icing. One was the Bindloss Marine Station while the other was Longo's Dock, owned by Antonio C. (Tony) Longo. Longo had taken over the operation on the old Railroad Wharf that had previously been used by Nat Avery, who attracted a significant number of boats during the 1920s. It was common for Stonington's many day boats to take out at these docks, tally their catch for later payment, and then the fish would be trucked away, principally to the Fulton Market each night. Longo also had equipment for taking out trash fish, and he operated Longo's Express for transporting market and trash fish. Through the decades, both the Longo and Bindloss facilities suffered wear and tear, and by the 1960s both were clearly in need of capital investment.[25]

After World War II, the Stonington fishing fleet numbered more than 50 vessels. Most of the draggers measured over 30 feet, with a design that had them low to the water and broad for their length. Two years after the war's end, about half of the fleet was powered by gasoline engines, the other half (generally the newer boats) by diesel. Internally, these efficient fishermen had a small combined cabin and galley forward, with from two to six bunks surrounding an oilcloth-covered table. Two benches and a coal stove completed the interior outfit, excepting the large pot of coffee that was, as on virtually all other American fishing vessels, always steaming on the stove.[26]

On deck, the typical Stonington dragger was clearly a descendant of the western-rig draggers of the 1920s. The forward pilothouse was set into the high foredeck that gave headroom to the cabin. A dory was often lashed atop the pilothouse as a lifeboat. Just aft of the house was the power take-off winch head and a mast and boom, all of which were used to manage the towing warps and haul the net aboard. The work deck aft was pierced with a hatch that led to the ice bin and fish hold. Known as "Stonington Draggers," these 55-foot workhorses were noted for their carrying capacity, sea-keeping ability, ruggedness, and economy of operation. Forty years later, many of the fishing vessels in the Borough were still those designed by Winthrop L. Warner and built at Henry R. Palmer's Stonington Boat Works during the early 1940s.[27]

The Warner-designed, Palmer-built vessels were not the only boats that made up the Stonington fleet at mid-century. Other boats were bought in neighboring ports and used in Stonington, including a few eastern-rig draggers, which veteran fishermen acknowledge can be a very sea-kindly boat. Another local designer was Ellery F. Thompson. A well-respected owner-captain and artist, Thompson fished out of the Borough for decades and also rendered oil paintings of local fishing

Aboard the *Eleanor* in 1945, Ellery Thompson prepares codfish cakes for the crew. The engine is under the table, with the chain drive for the trawl winch visable above Thompson's shoulder.
Gordon Sweet photograph.
Mystic Seaport 1989.108.2

With Captain Ellery Thompson by the *Eleanor's* wheel (right), crew members coil the towing warps as the trawl is hauled back. Gordon Sweet photograph. Mystic Seaport 1989.109.17

scenes, published two books, and designed fishing vessels. Thompson designs looked like the other western-rig draggers of southeastern Connecticut, but they included a number of modifications that Thompson's years on the after deck and in the pilothouse taught him would be of value. Some Ellery Thompson designs, like George Berg's *Old Mystic* and Peter Bessette's *Algarve* (ex-*New England*,) fished out of Stonington and other local ports until the end of the century. Meanwhile, Thompson's personality, experience, and flair for art and literature spread his reputation widely to, among others, readers of *The New Yorker* magazine.[28]

The fishing routine practiced by many of these Stonington vessels had been established long before the war, and it continues to the present day. Throughout the 1900s, Stonington draggers could be seen working "down the beach" just off the Rhode Island coast between Watch Hill and Point Judith. There, the draggers might catch spring haddock or flounder, summer fluke, flounder, or whiting, fall flounder or scup, and winter flounder, cod, or butterfish. Though often marketed as "sole" in stores and restaurants, five species of flounder —flukes, blackbacks, yellowtails, witches, and windowpanes —were regularly landed by Stonington men.

Other local grounds worked by the fleet included spots with evocative names: The Mouth south of the Thames River; Deep Water outside of Wicopesset Reef; Hell Hole north of Block Island; and Yellow Bank and the Mussel Bed off the Rhode Island shore. For decades, the "day boats" departed from Stonington each day before dawn to work these grounds, returning to port in the evening. Many of the larger vessels in the fleet became known as "trip boats" because they made trips lasting four to ten days as they sought their prey offshore or along the coast of New York, New Jersey, or Massachusetts. Meanwhile, the lobstermen of Stonington had innumerable sites where they could set their gear. Fishers Island Sound, with its many reefs and rock beds, offered a habitat that was ideal for lobstering. West of Fishers Island, the Race, with its deep reefs and swift-flowing tidal currents full of nutrients, was also a productive lobstering area.[29]

Fishermen "pick" the *Eleanor's* deck, sorting the catch.
Gordon Sweet photograph.
Mystic Seaport 1989.108.18

In 1949, Stonington's fishermen landed almost 15,000,000 pounds of fish, nearly 30 percent of which was shipped off and rendered down for animal feed. The highly prized yellowtail stocks had slipped however, as the landing of this species fell off sharply. At the same time, the state legislature in Hartford advanced plans to build a fish processing plant on Longo's Dock, and the residents of the Borough were threatened with the prospect of a fish plant in the heart of their community. The proposal for the plant was one of several efforts to reinvigorate the local fisheries from the postwar downturn. A study at that time determined that Stonington's fishermen were suffering the loss of between 30 and 90 percent of their gross receipts to high overhead and poor marketing. It was suggested that limited dock facilities, limited buyers, and the universal shipping of Stonington food fish to the Fulton Market placed the local draggermen at a great disadvantage. With the prospect of additional profits to the fishermen themselves of between $400,000 and $600,000 annually from the proposed processing plant, the debate regarding the facility was vital to both the fishing community and the village at large. The problem was that the potential smell from the fish plant would be the scent of money for those who made their living on the pier, but a nuisance odor that would likely result in reduced property values for hundreds of Borough homeowners. Ultimately, after much maneuvering in Stonington and in Hartford, it was determined

Ellery Thompson's 50-foot *Eleanor* was built at Delano, New Jersey, in 1927.
Mystic Seaport 1989.108.1

that a processing plant would not join the historic houses that populated the Borough. The fishing fleet would have to survive without the new facility.[30]

Even as the debate over the proposed plant raged, the fishermen of Stonington toiled on. In May of 1950, 36 draggers landed 518,400 pounds of fish. The highliner for the month was the *Carl J.*, which landed over 40,000 pounds of fish, while the *Fairweather* came in less than 1,000 pounds behind. In January of the next year, 37 draggers landed nearly 414,000 pounds of fish. The highliner for that month was George Berg's *Old Mystic*, bringing in 20,100 pounds of finfish from eight separate trips.[31]

By the end of the decade, more than 30 draggers, mostly in the 40-to-60-foot range, fished out of Stonington. Many were day boats that fished in Long Island Sound and Block Island Sound, boxing their catch onboard and delivering it at day's end. The trip boats at that time typically fished for two to five days in spots like the Gulley, out toward the edge of the continental shelf between the Hudson Canyon and Nantucket Shoals and 90 miles from port, where their otter trawls worked at depths of 50 to 70 fathoms (300 to 420 feet). At that time, the best catches were fluke from July through September, pogies through the summer, flounder in winter, and cod from November through February. Once the fish were landed, the boat owner took 40 percent of the receipts while the captain and crew of two or three men split the other 60 percent, as well as the "shack money" earned from selling baitfish or other incidentals of the catch at the dock. An annual income of $5,000 was considered good for a Stonington fisherman in the 1950s.[32]

Through much of the 1950s and on into 1970s, the Stonington fishermen were on hard times. A variety of factors combined to reduce the fleet significantly. Like many American fishermen, the men of Stonington witnessed foreign vessels working New England waters at unprecedented levels. Distant-water trawlers of the Soviet Bloc countries and European nations had begun to appear in the Western Atlantic in the 1950s, and their presence increased greatly in the 1960s. Fish stocks declined measurably as a result of this intensive fishing effort. At the same time, consumer preference for fish began to shift to the convenience of frozen white fish, often breaded and fried, reducing demand for some of the species landed in Stonington.

During these years the small, family owned draggers were unable to compete with this industrial approach to fish catching and processing. As a small port, Stonington's market share had, for years, relied on a cyclical harvest of a handful of valued species. The fluctuating seasonal landings of these fish, and their reduced stocks, combined with increasing competition in the waters fished by Stonington men, further challenged the Borough's fleet. As other southern New England ports like New Bedford, Massachusetts, and Galilee, Rhode Island, expanded their docking facilities, processing plants, and marketing methods, Stonington found itself at a disadvantage in the regional marketplace. Some local men either left the industry or moved their boats to those competing ports.[33]

By the early 1960s, only a handful of draggers worked out of the Borough.[34] For the next decade, the few remaining fishermen of Stonington, along with many of their New England brothers, continued to make their living from the sea, while ecological, market, and international developments made doing so increasingly difficult. Then, in 1976, the federal government stepped in to boost the fishing economy with the passage in Congress of the Magnuson Fishery Conservation and Management Act. This sweeping legislation established an exclusively

American economic zone within 200 miles of the coast and prohibited foreign-flag vessels from fishing within that zone unless licensed to do so. (State control of local waters was retained inside the three-mile limit.) On the heels of the Magnuson Act came the American Fisheries Promotion Act, which established a variety of funding sources to boost the size of the American fishing fleet.

The ensuing national boom in the fisheries included Stonington. Even before the Fisheries Promotion Act was in place, it was reported that 30 vessels, over half of which were lobster boats, worked out of the harbor. Already, the characteristic Stonington draggers were beginning to be replaced by a new style of fishing vessel. The first of these new vessels were directly inspired by the shrimp trawlers of the Gulf of Mexico, and some were actually built in the South. They were wide and shallow, with forward pilothouses like the western-rig boats. But they had two features not found on earlier Stonington boats. The first was the set of outriggers amidships designed for towing shrimp trawls. On the open sea, these long spars were also lowered to increase the vessel's stability, sometimes with a weighted "bird" hung off the end and submerged to reduce the rolling of the vessel.

The second feature of these new trawlers was a ramp cut into the stern for hauling the trawl aboard, with one or two hydraulic reels at the stern for winding in the net. Developed in Europe and on the West Coast in the 1950s, this style of net-handling increased both the efficiency and the safety of dragging.

The wooden shrimper-style boats were soon followed by large, rather boxy steel boats with pilothouse above a high foredeck. Aft, they had a well-sheltered working deck with stern ramp and net reels. These boats also used outriggers for stabilizing their relatively shallow hulls. They were driven by large diesel engines, equipped with well-insulated fish holds, and outfitted with surprising comfort and convenience, from TVs to refrigerators, in their spacious quarters forward. These large trawlers were the new generation of offshore trip boat, similar to the most modern boats in New Bedford, Gloucester, or other major fishing ports.

As these changes in the fleet were evolving, the selectmen of the Stonington calculated that, if the town's docks were repaired and upgraded, more large trawlers would join the fleet. Inadequate docking facilities had been one of the challenges faced by the Stonington fleet for some time. In the mid-1960s, Tony Longo offered to sell the old Steamboat Wharf to the town. If Stonington was going to own the wharf, improvements would have to be made to a facility that hadn't seen any significant capital investment in decades. With these changes in mind, the topic of a fish processing plant was floated once more. Once again, a number of the Borough residents voiced fears of the smell of a fish plant. On a number of occasions the small community's quiet fault line, which ran along the seams of class and ethnicity, spiced the debate over the uses of the wharf and its impact on the Borough as a whole. The earlier proposal for such a plant had resulted in the creation of the Stonington Welfare League, a residents' association that worked to protect the community and its property values from the smell of fish. It was clear that a processing plant would make the fishing port more competitive, but with real estate values rising, the value of property outweighed the value of the fishing industry and again the plan was denied.[35]

Just as the dynamic that boosted Nantucket's fishing industry 40 years earlier had boosted Stonington's, a similar pattern in real estate had evolved. Like its distant island neighbor, the Borough has remained insulated from significant change to its physical character for more than 150 years. During its heyday of whaling, sealing, and steamboating, Stonington saw nearly all of its buildable land put to use. Then, like that most famous of whaling ports, the Borough also found itself somewhat frozen in time. Nantucket had relied exclusively on whaling for its prosperity and fell into a slumber when that industry abandoned the island. Even though the local mills remained in operation, the Borough also saw its business decline when the night boats ceased running in 1904. And, although it was not located 30 miles at sea like Nantucket, Stonington Borough was far enough off the main transportation routes to remain a bit isolated, and insulated from intruders.

For the first half of the 1900s, many of the Borough's residents maintained their eighteenth- and nineteenth-century homes for one of two reasons. Either they appreciated and sought to maintain the community's historic character, or they could not afford to replace the old with the new, and simply maintained the aging structures in order to survive. As a result, the vast majority of the buildings standing south of the rail line had been built before 1900.[36]

The beauty of the Borough's setting, with open water on three sides, and with ancient homes lining the streets and alleyways throughout, created an appeal that had drawn comment for generations. With the completion of Interstate Highway 95 in the 1960s, access to the Borough from urban centers became more practical. The postwar economic boom had created extraordinary wealth for many residing in the greater New York area, which was only a few hours from Stonington by the Interstate. With highway access, Stonington became a weekend retreat and retirement community for the affluent. Within two decades, old houses valued at several thousand dollars became architectural gems that could command selling prices in the hundreds of thousands. Those prices continued to inflate during the ensuing years, and the homes in the village are now almost exclusively occupied by those who seek out, and can afford, the quaint charm of a small village frozen in time. As the financially secure moved in, the resultant change in demographics altered the nature of Stonington Borough more than anything since whaling days. And, although the commercial fishing fleet continues to operate at the Town Dock, the relationship between the fleet and the Borough has changed irreversibly. That change is also reflected in the out-migration of nearly all of those of Portuguese decent. This population, along with the Yankee fishermen with long-established roots in the region, made up the bulk of Stonington's fishing community.[37]

The first two Portuguese to come to the village were Frank G. Sylvia and Joseph A. Vargas, who arrived in Stonington in the 1840s and 1850s. Both were from the island of Fayal, in the Azores. In time, Vargas married Sylvia's eldest daughter, and the roots of a robust Portuguese destiny in Stonington were firmly planted. Other families followed during the next 100 years, and the names of Pont, Medeiros, Maderia, Souza, Luiz, Arruda, Silviera, Pacheco, Clay, Moniz, Amanico, Santos, Furtardo, Serrano, Almeida, Narcizzi, and others have been involved in all aspects of town life, including fishing, mill work, shop keeping, politics, and community service. The heart of that community's spiritual life was St. Mary's Roman Catholic Church, dedicated in 1851 for Stonington's Irish and adopted later by the Portuguese.[38]

Many Portuguese had fished in the old country and came to the New World to practice their skills in a more promising environment. Family members who came to Stonington brought others over and supported them as they struggled to become established and secure a future for their children.[39] It should be remembered that an important part of Stonington's story is its role in this nation's greatest maritime and human accomplishment: transatlantic migration.

This migration sometimes led to tensions along the seams of race, ethnicity, and faith. In small, compact, and isolated Stonington Borough, one could expect these seams to be exposed on a regular basis. And so they were when the question of fish processing came up. An observer reported a clear ethnic divide between the descendents of Northern Europeans and the Portuguese. One Portuguese referred to "them uptown," meaning the Anglos who lived in the larger homes with their groomed lawns up on Main Street. Meanwhile, some "nativists" might lob disparaging slurs at the Portuguese who lived in the much less elegant, much more compressed section of the village down near the point. These differences, which usually remained latent, might briefly boil to the surface when political or economic issues came into play. Otherwise, these differences had little effect on daily life. As Ellery Thompson put it, people were more interested in the quality of one's neighbors than in their origins. Some of Stonington's most respected and best-liked draggermen were Portuguese. Those who grew up in the Borough and worked on the draggers also reported that ethnicity and national origin meant little. Children's play groups and fishing crews alike paid little attention to one's faith, ethnic group, or primary language.[40]

At the same time, the Portuguese residents enriched the religious and cultural life of the community and gave it open expression through events like the annual Blessing of the Fleet and the Feast of the Holy Ghost (celebrating the end of a famine in medieval Portugal and put on by Stonington's Holy Ghost Society, founded in 1914). The first of these events was connected exclusively to the fishing industry. Portuguese fishermen in Gloucester and other New England ports had begun annual blessing-of-the-fleet ceremonies early in the 1900s, and Stonington's fleet began the ceremony in the mid-1950s. It has remained an important part of the Borough's summer calendar ever since. Steeped in the authority of the Holy Roman Catholic Church, the Blessing has been strongly supported by the Portuguese members of the fishing community, if not by their Protestant counterparts.[41]

Throughout the first half of the 1900s, the Portuguese and their Yankee neighbors lived together in the Borough, and both languages could be heard on the streets and in the shops. By mid-century, those of Portuguese descent made up over half of Stonington's fishermen. Their stories are those shared by their Yankee brethren, but also reflect the strong sense of family and faith that are so central to the Portuguese character.[42]

Manuel Roderick came to Stonington from Terceira, the Azores, in 1907. He fathered 14 children in Stonington. Eight of the young Rodericks were male; all became fishermen. Perhaps the most dramatic event in that family's fishing life occurred in February of 1945. Captain Manuel had lost both of his legs years earlier and commanded his 55-foot *Alice and Jenny* by being lashed to the chair at the wheel as two of his sons worked the deck. While struggling through a blizzard, the vessel grounded off Block Island. Cutting their father free of his chair, the two Roderick boys fought their way clear of the wreck. Captain Manuel was lowered onto his son George's back, and the three fishermen battled through the icy seas as the snow whistled by in the five-degree temperature. Eventually the three family members made their way ashore, and then overland to Old Harbor, where they arrived, cold but alive.[43]

Such disasters in heavy weather were a constant threat. If treacherous weather passed through, those on shore were doomed to wait in uncertainty until word of the fate of loved ones became known. Through much of the twentieth century, limited communications left Stonington fishing families, Portuguese and Yankee alike, fearing the worst long after the danger had passed. In March of 1917, the friends and family of Captain Manuel Maderia prayed for his return when his dory went missing in the fog and snow eight miles southwest of Watch Hill. Earlier in the afternoon, Connie Maderia had, with a fisher wife's observant eye, sensed impending peril. As the winter light faded and fuel ran low, Maderia's crew had been forced to break off their search and motored to the Borough without their captain. They, and others, would return to the fishing grounds the next morning to continue their search. Meanwhile, throughout the evening the Maderia women and children fervently prayed for his safe return. With no sign of Maderia all the following day, his wife donned the black dress of a widow. As the household went into mourning, scores of people from all strata of the community came to the house to pay their respects and offer support for the bereft young family.

Unbeknownst to any of them, Manny Maderia had been driven west by the storm and fought his way to Gardiner's Island, where he landed, cold, wet, and without shelter. Two days after going missing, and after great suffering from cold, exhaustion, and frostbite, Maderia made his way to Oyster Ponds on the north fork of Long Island, where he was taken in by a shoreside family. A telegram reached Stonington four days after the trial had begun. The Maderia children were no longer fatherless, and Connie would have her husband back. True to the character of a fishing community, neighbors brought clothing and food to the Maderias, understanding that a man who had barely survived such an ordeal would need time to mend before he could again go to sea.[44]

Nearly 40 years later, a similar incident took place when Hurricane Carol forced Charles Fellows and his dragger in from "the corner," a section of fishing grounds near the Nantucket lightship. As Fellows motored through the rising storm to seek shelter in Vineyard Sound, he listened to the final radio transmissions of an eastern-rig dragger that had chosen to run across Nantucket Shoals. Her 11-man crew never saw home. Fellows and his crew, however, rode Carol out just off Oak Bluffs, Martha's Vineyard. But, the hurricane destroyed the region's telephone and electrical systems, leaving Betty Fellows without word of her husband's fate. Three days passed, and Betty began to believe she was a widow, and contemplated how to support her young children alone. The following day, when Charlie motored around the Point and up to Longo's Dock, it seemed that the whole town was there to welcome the crew home. Betty recalls being nearly as angry as she was relieved with the safe return of her husband.[45]

Of course not every close call ended in relief and a warm embrace. Currently, 37 names are etched in the granite Stonington Fishermen's Memorial on the end of the Town Dock. Each of those names represents a life cut short, taken by the sea and lost to those held dear. As is true in other fishing communities around the globe, the families and friends of Stonington's fishermen have endured the sorrow of loss. So it was with the destruction of the dragger *Nathaniel Palmer*, which in the winter of 1945 brought World War II ordnance to the surface entangled in her net. The ensuing explosion destroyed the *Palmer*, killing Captain Bob Moran and all but one of his crew. Aboard the *New England*, when Arthur Arruda was carried overboard by the towing warps, he was last seen far below the surface while kin on deck, who were also family, watched helplessly. George Roderick, who had carried his father to safety through Block

Island's icy seas, died on the afterdeck of a vessel named after his own daughter when a careening block struck him in the head. And howling wind and snow ashore were a portent of sorrow when the offshore lobster boat *Heidi Marie* went missing with all hands. An exhaustive search by the Coast Guard turned up no sign of her crew.[46]

Through the latter part of the twentieth century, the Stonington fishing fleet continued to put to sea, and the memory of those lost lived on. But even as the fishing saga continued, the community from which it set out changed significantly. Rising real estate values and an influx of older, financially secure residents represented a shift in the community's character and identity. The changing character of the Borough population is evident in hard numbers as well as in the memories of local residents over the last half century.

In the 1950s, 1,760 individuals lived in the village. Many of those residents were members of large and extended Portuguese families. The connection between these extended families and the Borough's fishing community was well established. One study found that, of the Stonington fishermen interviewed, 62 percent were Portuguese, while 60 percent came to their fishing career through their father. Overall, 71 percent came to fishing through kin or had kin working in the fleet along with them. So, for more than two-thirds of the fishermen, family and fishing could not be separated.[47]

Built for John Bindloss, the 47-foot western-rig dragger *Little Chief* was launched by Henry Palmer at Stonington in 1945. She lies at Longo's Dock in this 1955 photograph.
Mystic Seaport 1988.16.19

Even while those familial connections to the fishing industry remained, the Borough's population continued to decline. By 1980, the population was down to 1,228 people, and it continued to slide to only 1,100 in 1990. Those who knew the village and its fishing community understood why this drastic reduction had taken place. As Captain George Berg put it, increased taxes and growing property values, combined with the mobility afforded by owning a car, impelled the

Portuguese of the Borough to out-migrate to Pawcatuck or to other nearby residential areas. There, the sudden appreciation in value of their Borough homes could be reinvested in an older Pawcatuck house or a ranch house in a new development. As a result, where once they could walk down to the boats at the dock, they now commuted to work in their pickup trucks just like their neighbors in other occupations.

It was all over by the 1980s, said Berg. In 1993, Captain Walter Allyn noted that very few fishermen lived in the Borough. Now it was the "affluent people" who inhabited the community. Captain James Henry, who had been an officer for the Southern New England Fishermen's and Lobstermen's Association as far back as the 1950s, said that two-thirds of the fishermen lived right in the Borough back then. That was until "big money came for the houses, then everybody wanted to get away from it." Perhaps no one could better chronicle the exodus of Stonington Borough's Portuguese and other fishing families than Captain Manny Maderia, the aging son of Manuel and Connie Maderia who had suffered so much 70 years before. Maderia, who still helped his own son, Captain Richard Maderia, prepare his lobster bait, saw increased property values as the cause for the change in demographics. "I may be the only Portuguese fisherman left in town," he said in 1993.[48]

By the late 1970s, there were 2,200 linear feet of mooring space between the two piers at the town dock. There was also an icehouse, a fuel storage depot, and an off-loading facility where the catch was landed, washed, and boxed for transport. The town of Stonington owned the pier facilities and leased them to the Southern New England Fishermen's and Lobstermen's Association. While the town was responsible for public access to the area, the Association attended to the sublet portions of the facility to the product buyers. Two buyers, Connecticut Seafoods and Stonington Fillet Company, competed for the fleet's take. At the same time, the Fishermen's and Lobstermen's Association provided a dockmaster to oversee operations at the dock. But in most respects the facilities had not changed significantly since the town purchased the property years before.[49]

Improvements came during the 1980s, when the state of Connecticut proffered over $600,000 to upgrade the Town Dock. The enhancements included the construction of a 50-by-120-foot steel building into which fish could be off-loaded. During the 1930s and 1940s, there had a filleting plant in the Borough. One returned after a 20-year absence (Stonington Fillet Company), but plans in the early 1980s to expand the fish processing operations were opposed by residents. Additional ideas for further development of the fishing facility have conflicted with proposals for alternative uses of the waterfront. A particular example of this was the tension surrounding the development of condominiums just to the south of the Town Dock, on the site of the old Stonington Boat Works yard. The discussions about the use of this site were contentious, and the construction of the condominiums themselves was not universally welcomed.[50]

In the early 1980s, 16 trip boats made up Stonington's offshore fleet. By 1985, between lobstermen, day boats, and trip boats, the fleet numbered nearly 40 vessels. Of these, 11 were lobster boats of varying sizes and 16 were draggers measuring between 40 and 60 feet. The average age of these draggers was 31 years, and although the newer vessels were fiberglass or steel, the majority of them were still wooden. The landings for 1985 totaled 3,000,000 pounds of fin- and shellfish. This equaled 68 percent of the state's total landings of finfish. Many of the predominant species being off-loaded in the Borough were familiar to generations of Stonington fishermen. They included lobster, blackback and yellowtail flounders, whiting, butterfish, and scup. Swordfish were always a valuable summer product as well. This growth in vessel numbers reflected the expanding American fisheries on the heels of the Magnuson Act and the American Fisheries Promotion Act.[51]

As the decade of the 1980s came to a close, the fishermen of Stonington continued to set out in search of nature's bounty. The fishing community of Long Point had seen challenges and changes throughout its more than two centuries of history. Hurricanes, migrations in and out, tragedy, and the endless cycles of economy and fish stocks had all been weathered by the generations of men and women of the Stonington fishing community. Yet new, and perhaps more harrowing, challenges had been developing. With the expansion of America's (and the world's) fisheries came additional pressure on fish populations. In many cases, a growing fleet, combined with refinements and advances in technology, had begun to overwhelm the natural stocks. Decreases in fish populations resulted in increased governmental involvement in the industry. By the 1990s, government regulations designed to protect fish stocks, combined with increasing overhead costs and reduced catches, became the most important challenges yet to the Stonington's fleet. The ever-changing story of Stonington and its fishermen was destined to encompass these new challenges even as the ever-constant challenges of the sea awaited.

GLENN S. GORDINIER

Jenna Lynn, 2004

Fishermen's Work

John DeBragga mending a net.

Day Boat Routine

Miss Karyn.

The fishermen's daily routine begins in darkness, especially for the smaller draggers or "day boats." The fishermen drive to the dock, typically arriving about 4:00 A.M. The day boats are generally manned by a captain, who is usually the boat owner, and one crew member. They prepare for their trip and set out from Stonington Harbor in the early morning darkness. Their departure is timed so that they will begin fishing at or near first light. Unless the ocean is shrouded in clouds, their day often begins with the dramatic sight of the sun rising over the water. It is a spectacular experience, but the romance of the moment is soon subdued by the odors of diesel fumes and kerosene heaters, the rumble of the boat's engine, and the churning sounds of the net reel and winches. The work of fishing begins.

When they arrive at their preferred fishing grounds, the boats "set their gear" and begin the first of the day's several tows. They haul a large net called an otter trawl across the ocean floor, with the boat moving at a very slow rate of speed. The net is about 100' long and about 90' wide. Long towlines called warps attach the net to the boat. Large metal doors attached to the warps near the wings of the trawl provide the pressure to keep the net open as it moves through the water. A tow usually lasts for two or three hours. Then the men haul the net back and empty it on the deck. They sort the catch, discarding unmarketable fish and stowing the fish that will be kept in the boat's hold.

A typical day for a small dragger consists of three tows. Upon completion of the final tow, the boat heads for home. The men process the fish, or "pick the deck," from the last tow as the boat makes its way back towards Stonington. This return trip can last several hours, depending upon where the men have been fishing on that day.

To work safely, efficiently, and enjoyably on a day boat, the captain and crew member develop a close relationship. For extended periods they may spend as much time with each other as they do with their families. They learn to accommodate to each other's habits, anticipate each other's actions, and to pace the work smoothly. Flexibility is another important quality, and is central to the fishing life.

"Right now we're in the dead of winter here. We listen to the weather forecast several times a day. It changes just about every time you hear it. So you don't know if you are coming or going. You try to plan your day accordingly, well you finally make up your mind. The next morning you get up about three o'clock, you look outside. If it's windy, you stay home; if it's not, you go. There are no fish inshore right now. We stay inshore off the beaches where we can just stay close to land and the weather doesn't affect us much. But there isn't any reason to go there because we check it and there are no fish there at all. Not enough to even pay expenses. So we have to travel 12, 15, 20 miles away, and you've got to have pretty good days to get out there. So, the day starts about three o'clock, you go down to the dock, you get in your boat. It is about a two-hour ride out to the grounds to get where we are going, and we sit out there and fish all day long providing the weather cooperates with us. We make long tows; three hours, four hours sometimes. We're on the deck sometimes 45 minutes to an hour, usually less than that. We love to be out on the deck because that is the only time we are making any money. Usually we'd spend like three tows a day. Now in the summertime, the hours aren't much different; we get up early because daylight is much earlier even though we are fishing close to home. We want to get out there at the crack of dawn, or even get the first tow in the darkness most of the time. That is when you get the best fish is your early morning drag. And it is probably the same routine, you just go through the motions all day long, although we do better; get more species of fish. That is when you get the warm water bringing all the different species in. It is a little more critical, I'd say, as far as the money-making aspect of it. Because that is about the only time we do anything at all. Usually 4:00 or 5:00 in the afternoon we are already in. The day's long enough when you start at three in the morning.

There is plenty of daylight left; you probably should be out there till dark because that is when you get a chance to make some money. But it gets to you after a while. You do probably six days a week. Some of these guys fish seven. I take Sundays off. Some of these guys go day in and day out. You are going to get a bad day, a bad-weather day or something's going to break, something needs to be repaired and that falls in all the time. Hopefully you are financially able to have it fixed and do it right. This time of the year, we are taking a heck of a gamble. Even if we do get out, we are barely making ends meet. If something goes wrong, that's just about it."

Tim Medeiros

Seafarer deck view.

"

Sometimes they go in for lobster bait, and they catch more skates in the dark, so they want to make that first tow in the dark in the deep water to catch skates for lobster bait. So, they'll leave two thirty, three o'clock. Other times, of course, it's easier to set in the daylight. So, if they leave here by five o'clock, they're there by first light to set the net.

Dick Bardwell

We go on the boat and have a bowl of cereal or a doughnut and coffee, or something, and a sandwich for lunch.

John Rita

Most of the time, in my boat, we bring your own. Whatever you want to eat, you bring for yourself for the day. If we're just day-fishing. We usually don't have a breakfast, or you pick up some donuts or something.

Tim Madeiros

It's seven days a week. You're working from 8:30 in the morning till noon, at least. And my friends would have Friday night, they'd all go out. I might go out with them until nine o'clock, and then it was time for me to go home. You don't have a whole heck of a lot of social life, and I think that's why fishermen band together when they're at the dock. That's their time to be social. And you need your sleep. You can't really do too much else.

Michael Medeiros

You are always thinking. You've got to watch out for things. There are a lot of things down there that if you fetch up your net on, you could rip it to pieces or you could lose it all. If you lose it all, you might as well hang it up these days. You are talking five or six thousand dollars to replace what you've got down there if not more. It is not a game. The other guy, he has nothing to lose, maybe a couple of days. He knows that if something happened, I am going to fix it. That is just the way that is. There are other boats, they might demand a little bit more from their crewmen. There might be a lot more involved. Some boats, that's all they do is rip nets, day in and day out. These guys have got to know how to fix them, or they don't get jobs.

Tim Medeiros

Anything happens, I mean it's just like having a brother or a father or whatever on the boat. It's funny how all of a sudden you're working with this guy so long every thought is the same, every movement is the same. You go to grab a knife, you both grab it, it's unbelievable.

Al Maderia

"

Tim Medeiros.

"

We all fished in the same areas. And there's a lot of camaraderie, joking around, helping each other on shore. You know, if somebody's having trouble with his net, another fisherman might lend him a spare net, just to see if it'll work out. They'll give away a lot of their secrets on shore.

When you're out fishing it's a different story. People are always switching from one [CB] channel to another, especially with my father and John operating two boats that work side by side. They'd speak in code. And you would rarely let someone know that you found fish, because there was so little of it that you wanted to be a little bit selfish with it. And you might go home that night and call up the same person that you were trying to pull one over on, and you might tell him that night, "We found flounder, and it was in back of the reef." Or it was wherever. So, it's a very distinct line between when you will help somebody and when you won't.

Michael Medeiros

We are usually fishing in the same grounds more or less. I can't say that we are really cooperative towards one another, I mean, somebody finds a little bit of fish a lot of times and it is kind of hush-hush. Of course it is not a big secret when you come in at night and somebody is going to find out that you've caught some fish. And then we get into the name-calling bit. We stay on the CB sets most of the day, and we call each other names and sandbaggers and kidding around mostly, just something to pass the time of day, because there really isn't that much work to be done out there anymore. That's it you know, we kind of all grew up together, we're friends. We certainly wouldn't do anything to hurt one another. When it comes down to the brass tacks, we're together. There are a couple there that, they say, "Well, what's mine is mine and to heck with anybody else." But you are going to find that no matter where you go.

Tim Medeiros

"

John Rita taking out.

"

Fluke come in first week in May, like clockwork. They'll come through. Like last year, the first weeks of May, we had to throw them away; we couldn't keep them. They had the ban on them. So we were throwing away a couple hundred bucks a day worth of food probably. Then after they kind of moved in, then you don't see them. You get a few here and there, but you don't really work on them. That is when we get our flounder run. They start picking up in April a little bit, and through May. Memorial Day, that's when they really boom. All at once they're here. And we go crazy. We're out fishing on them left and right. We don't get much else. We get a little bit of squid.

Usually in July, end of June, the fishing is done. Then personally I'll go fluke fishing up in the Sound off of New London, on down, way down, off New Haven and places like that. A lot of guys don't bother doing that because there's not a lot of fluke, but it is tricky fishing. You've got to get into some pretty tight spots. And it is boring. You don't get anything else. You tow for hours and hours, and you might get a basket of fluke. I don't know. Some guys just lay up their boats, paint them during that time, and wait for the fall run. I just keep going myself. I keep plugging. I can't afford to stay home.

We are like clockwork too. We have logbooks that we keep all the time, tell us where we fished, and certain times of the year, what we've caught there so we can go back. It is usually pretty in range. Some species, I should say. Not all species. Sometimes you can just take the logbook and throw it away, because it is not going to do you any good.

Tim Medeiros

"

Lobster Boat Routine

Lobster pot identification plate.

The daily routine for lobstermen is different. They focus their work around their essential piece of gear, the lobster pot. It is a rectangular trap, made of vinyl-covered heavy wire mesh, which is baited with various types of fish. A net known as a funnel is placed inside the pot at the opening, enabling lobster to get in, but not out. The pots are strung together in groups of as many as 20, known as trawls. Buoys attached to the trawl mark its location.

Usually two men go out on lobster boats, although lobstermen sometimes work alone. The lobstermen must work with the tides, setting and hauling their gear in harmony with the changing ocean currents caused by the rising and falling tides. Newly baited pots are carried out to the lobstermen's preferred area and set. After several days, lobstermen return to haul their gear, generally during slack tide. A pot hauler, a powered winch hanging at the rail near the boat's wheel, makes it easy for the lobstermen to haul the trawl of pots up from the bottom. Lobsters are measured, and if of legal length, their claws are banded and they are placed in a tank of water. The pots are then baited and reset in the same area. The pace of setting and hauling is quick.

The lobsterman's scheduled is influenced by the number of lobster pots he is fishing. Deck space is limited, even on the large 45-foot lobster boats, so on a good day a lobster boat may make several trips back and forth to the Town Dock.

"

Probably, during the summer months, it is get up by four o'clock. Usually get up by four. Out on the water by 4:30 at the latest. Lucky if you're home in bed by eight, 8:30 at night. Because we wouldn't get in a lot of times until three, four o'clock in the afternoon. Full day. And by the time you get the bait, get enough of it done so you have a jump on it for the next day. Back then I fished a lot of times alone. Didn't have a deckhand. Finally did get a deckhand when I could get one. A lot of times I fished alone which probably wasn't a good thing, but I did.

Wooden pots seem to be a little less efficient compared to the wires. Hauling the wire pots is easier on your body. I'm sure I have a lot more ailments, aches and pains because of the physical part of it with the wooden pots and putting the two-and-a-half-gallon pail of cement in them to make them sink. And once they get waterlogged they would be heavier and there was a lot more physical work with the wooden pots. It's a little easier with the wire ones. I guess it was the late eighties I started switching over. I tried 50 one year. I had some combination pots first: wooden frames, wire sides. They seemed to work pretty well maintenance-wise, repair-wise. And then I bought, I think, 50 to try. And then I knew from that point that I was going to pursue it, if nothing else, for my summertime activities just because it was easy to move more gear faster with wire pots. And I think I purchased 500 or 800 right after that. The first ones I bought, I still have some of them to this day.

Sizes and funnels, lengthwise we ended up with a 36-inch pot. I've tried the four-footers, the five-footers when I was fishing wood. And then we went into the wire; we did 36 by 12 by 20. And now we decided to go something a little bit wider, I think they're 22 or 21 1/2. And they're 36 long and 13 1/2 inches high. Just seems to be a better-all-around pot for fishing the three or four different areas that I fish. Spring, summer, and fall there. And during the winter. Just an all-around pot. And they stack all the same on the boat when they're the same size. You know, when you're setting it's important that they're all stackable; you need uniform stuff to stack in set loads.

Mike Grimshaw

"

Mike Grimshaw.

"

I fish a 42-foot boat to the fullest capacity. I have 3,000 pots, all wire. We haul about 600 pots a day. My style of fishing's totally different from when I started out. I fished almost all singles back then; now I fish all trawls. I don't have any singles. People still fish singles around me but it's just inefficient. Too many turns.

I have places that I fish six-pot trawls because that's the scope of the bottom and the rock piles. So, six would be pretty efficient across the rocks. And offshore the bottom's a lot more open and softer and different kind of style of fishing. We fish 20-pot trawls in one area because that's the length of the ground. Instead of putting two tens, it's just a lot easier to put one twenty. Because we can handle them on the rail, on the stern, the way we stack them.

The pot-hauler could haul a hundred if I had some place to stack them. I did try one 35 trawl. It's just a nuisance to pile all the rope up on deck underneath the hauler, and where are you going to put all the pots on the rail to set them? The trawl size I like to fish is about a 13-pot trawl. Nobody likes that number, but it works for me. Twelve pots all the way down my rail and across my stern, and the last pot's up there with me at the davit and the wheel. I fish loran lines now. I push it off and it self-sets the rest of it. Nobody has to do anything. They either band or gauge lobsters. Totally out of the way of harm. So, it's a little easier. With a 20-pot trawl they've got to set the first six or five pots. I think it's six. I set the first, but they still got to set five pots. And then the rest self-sets after that.

Most of the time there's about 20 fathom [120 feet of line] between the pots, as a rule. Fifteen or twenty fathom. Depends where I'm at. Inshore ones, I'm a little closer. The offshore ones I'm about 20 fathom apart. Inshore, I use sinking nylon, like a dacron or a nylon, and offshore all poly [polypropylene]. Offshore I fish Block Island Sound, west of Montauk, east of the [Fishers] Island, west of Block Island. And then I have a set I push up inshore in the summer time where I fish during the winter. During the winter and fall I fish down from like the Rhode Island border to, I bump into the New York border, right down to like Groton Long Point or something like that, or the Dumplings there, North and South Dumpling. That's where I fish during the winter. And then during the spring I fish up as far as Plum Island, coming back through to like Ocean Beach, out in the Race, Middle Race they call it. That's where I fish during the spring.

Mike Grimshaw

"

Setting a trawl from *Lady Lynn*.

"

There are two phases of the operation during the wintertime. In the fall it's just me and my younger stepson, Nathan. I gaff the buoy and run it up to the first pot. I break it, turn it, he takes it to the stern, cleans it out, stacks it while I'm running up the next one to the rail. And I break it and bring it in. And he takes it to the stern. Once we get the trawl up–whether it's six, ten, or whatever it is–I turn and set it, and while I'm doing that he's gauging through all the lobsters and banding them. He cleans the pots out in the stern and puts them in a tote, what he thinks to be legal. Throws over the eggers and shorts, if it's obvious, when he's cleaning out the pots. And then he'll go through what he saved in the tote while I'm setting out the trawl.

And we change it a little bit in the summertime, when I have a third man with me, counting myself. All he does is, when I break the pot, he runs the pot from where I am to the stern where Nathan is so Nathan can just clean out the pot, the lobsters, and bait it, stack it. And the other fellow just comes back up to where I am to receive the next one. Because where I fish offshore, the bottom's pretty clean and free of hangs and snags. And I usually have the hauler running at full capacity, maxed out. Probably my name should have been Max.

We can haul a trawl of 13 pots offshore in about five minutes. That's up, down, turn and set it. I don't say that's the first trawl in the morning when everybody's kind of looking for a rhythm, but when everybody's in their rhythm and doing what they're supposed to be doing, and I'm making that hauler crank, the guy that runs the pot from where I am to the stern, he should have tennis shoes on or jogging shoes, he shouldn't have boots.

About time we hit Napatree buoy he lets the water out of the tanks and starts emptying out the tanks, separating them out from two claws to culls so by the time we get to the dock he's ready to take them right off and go into the buyer with them versus sitting at the dock waiting to take them up to him. This way here, on the way in we keep them wet, take them right out. Get it done quick so we can either get our bait or go home.

It's still $3.25 a pound, but we never went below that this summer. Last winter we were up as high as I think $6.50 or $6.75. Seven fifty was the most we got two years ago during the winter. Which was pretty nice. But you're not getting much. You're only getting probably a hundred pounds. Just makes it workable for you to go all winter to get that hundred pounds a day. That's what we strive for. In the dead of winter, if we can get a hundred pounds and the price is $6.00, $7.00 a pound then everybody gets something out of it.

"

Mike Grimshaw

Manny Maderia.

"

Probably over half of it is tides. We get a little bit of break when we go offshore in the summertime. The tides are a little lazier outside compared to in close to land. Some places we definitely need the slack for a couple hours or an hour and a half before the slack. Other places we don't need any at all, offshore. Inside, and then during the spring and during the winter and that, you've got to be right on it or you're wasting your time. You lose efficiency as far as getting up the maximum number of pots or a certain amount. You should be getting up ten to fifteen trawls, and you go out there and get seven because you came too late. And if you go out there too early–which happens sometimes, but you try to bear in mind "better early than late"–you sit there for an hour and a half not doing anything. But hopefully you've got some bait to string or something.

I just kind of scratch it [my schedule] out on the dash or something. Dash of the boat that we're going to be here today. And if it's a place where I'm going to fish tides then I know I can get two or three tides in a day, because the daylight's longer. I fish usually two of those kind of places a day, even though I have three places like that that I fish during the summer. And I try to alternate them so they're kind of not conflicting with the rest of them. With the rest of the areas.

In January we're finishing up from the fall run. Probably dies out by the end of January. Maybe into the first week of February that you get a fair amount, you know, few hundred pounds a day or something. And then at that point we're bringing gear in that we fished during the fall. So, by February, the end of it, we're definitely weeding out the dead wood where the run lobsters don't come through anymore, the stuff that's not on the hard bottom. And thinking about where we're going in March, which would be the Race, up to the westward. And we start setting up there anytime by the end of February to the first of March. And I stay there until the end of May, though I'm not totally out of there by the end of May. End of May, I go to Block Island. So then I'm running two and a half hours from that point to the point I fish to the eastward. So, one day I might be going west where I'm fishing the tides. The next day I might be going east where I'm not fishing the tide. And just on top of that I might be going south where I need the tide to set pots inside. Some days I don't know what direction we're going in. And we fish that way until about sometime in the middle of September, offshore and inshore. And we get out of the Race by usually the middle of June. By the fifteenth I try to be out of there. And we stay out in Block Island [Sound] until, well, the latest I've been there was like October 31st. And then, we start back inshore again.

"

Mike Grimshaw

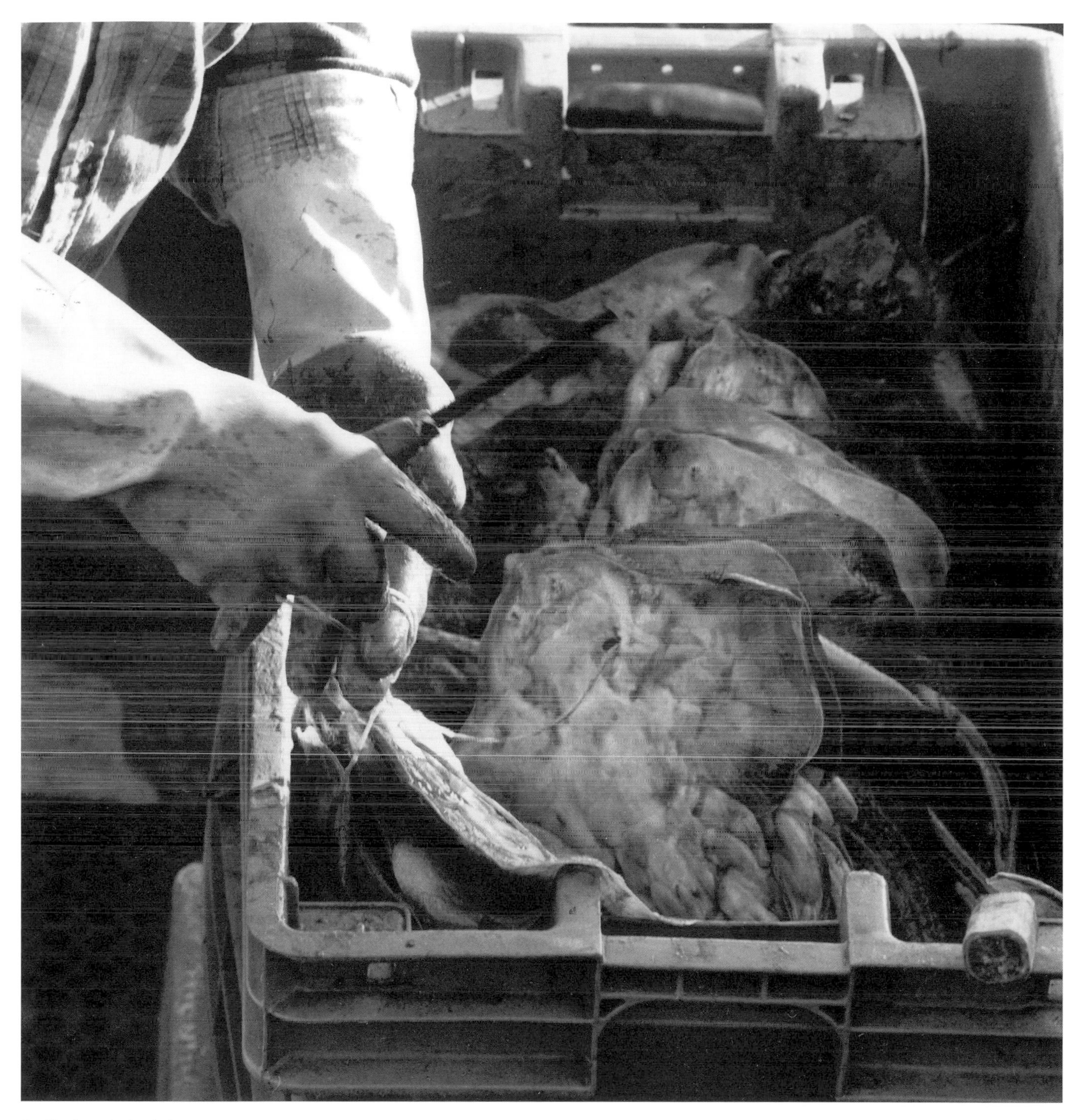

Joe Kessler stringing bait.

"

In the beginning of the year, summer, we'll just haul. Eat a sandwich or some kind of junk food on the fly or a soda. Way back when, I never used to bring anything. If I had a can of soda on the boat it was a miracle. We didn't have water. Then I started bringing my kids with me and I just start thinking, "Oh, gee, I've got to give them a soda or give them something to eat." Because it's a long day, you know. Yourself, you're old enough so you can understand, you don't worry about it, think about it, you just do it. With the kids you get a little more conscious. Their mother started packing them a lunch and got into the routine. We fell right into that. But now, I mean, towards the middle of the summer there, when you start to get a little more fatigued, everybody gets a little bit worn, then, yeah, I'll throw it out of gear for ten minutes or something. Everybody will have a sandwich or a drink or whatever's necessary. Unless we're fishing some place that doesn't allow it, like a tide or something or a couple of those places we have a slack that there's no way we can take a break in the middle of it. We've got to keep going. But then there's usually an hour ride in or an hour and a half ride out or whatever.

Mike Grimshaw

Roderick Grimshaw

"

Trip Boat Routine

The offshore draggers, or trip boats, leave the dock on fishing trips lasting from a few days to ten days or more. They normally carry a crew of four or five men, with one serving as cook. Their extended absence from their Stonington base also requires that they depart well stocked with fuel, food, and ice. They often time their departure so they arrive on the fishing grounds in the early morning light, following a trip that may take 14 hours or more.

Because they fish in significantly deeper waters than their inshore counterparts, their trawl gear, including net and wire cables, my extend nearly a half mile. They often make tows lasting four or five hours, and they may fish around the clock. Their catch is well iced down in the hold of the vessel to insure its preservation. During their down-time they eat well, read, or watch videos. It may take a half day or more for a trip boat to return to the Town Dock from the offshore fishing grounds.

Jim Allyn.

"

In the early days, I think we'd take aboard what we wanted under both arms. But you've got to remember one thing, the trips weren't as long, either. Three, four days; maybe five. Now, twelve, thirteen days is nothing. What determines your length of the trip today isn't the perishable item you're putting in the fish hold, it's how much fuel you've got. Because these boats are very well equipped to carry that cargo, with the insulation they have.

Walter Allyn

Everybody's got their own way of doing it, I guess. But myself, we've been pretty versatile, I guess you'd say. Starting with the first of the year, in the winter, in January through March we concentrate on summer flounder or fluke. It's been our big game, and we've fished them around the Hudson, anywhere from Hudson Canyon all the way east down to Munson Canyon. That's down south, southeast of Nantucket, a hundred and fifty miles or so. It's the southern edge of Georges Bank; it's the continental shelf, runs down to the east, down towards the Canadian line there and it be the southern half of the bank itself, Georges Bank. Where the Hudson Canyon is right south of Long Island, out that way.

And we'll start, the first of the year, up around the Hudson and by the latter part of the spring there, you're out towards the Munson Canyon area. Down east, follow the fish. And then, after that, we come into April. I might do a monkfish trip or something like that and then we'd be switching over to go scalloping. And what I do then is take all my nets off, take all the doors off. We take them off and put on the steel dredges and I'll fish doing that right up till say October. And then I'll go back dragging again.

They're long trips; they're ten days. Ten-day trips. We try to run our schedule where we get two trips a month. So we'll fish ten days, take out on the eleventh, take four off, and leave on the fifth day. That will make up your thirty days, in a month, if you try to keep the schedule. In the summer you don't really worry too much about weather and all of that. Got a good schedule in the summer, where in the wintertime, you know, you kind of come and go with the weather. It's difficult. Like this time of year now the weather's changing, you get the big winds.

Jim Allyn

"

Approaching the dock.

"

The mate, he takes the boat over; he runs the whole show when I'm in the bunk. The engineer, he takes care of the engine; he's down there pumping bilges. He puts oil in the motors. Every four hours he's down there just even taking a spot check. The fish-hold man, he's in charge of taking care, making sure the fish hold's balanced out with the engineer as far as ice, fish. You've got to keep her straight. You don't want the boat listing to one side or the other; you want to keep the boat as straight as you can. So he works with the engineer a lot of times. The engineer will switch the fuel over to burn off the port side, where the fish-hold man might be putting fish on that same side. Putting fish down on the port, so you're putting weight on the port side, and your're taking weight off the port side with fuel. So they kind of work together, very vital that you keep the boat straight. You don't want to list. Makes it very uncomfortable with a list. You're all laid over one way, rolling around. It's uncomfortable and hard to handle gear. It's dangerous too.

Jim Allyn

Well, let's say, right now we're monkfishing, so, we'll say we usually have between four or five guys, depending. You'll know how much you're going to catch, basically. And you know how many guys you need where you can still make money. So, you take either four or five guys. All the gear's ready, you're fueled up, iced up, you know, all the food's on board. You leave, the captain will usually drive the boat outside. Sometimes we'll leave at night, like in the evening, early evening, to get there for, say, the next morning. You can start fresh in the morning, fresh start. It's usually between 12 and 16 or 18 hours to get to the grounds.

So, you usually leave Stonington. Captain will usually hold the wheel until maybe we get outside of Montauk. Just like 13 or 15 miles from here. And then, after that if he wants to lay down or whatever, you start running a watch, a wheel watch, between the four guys, if the four guys are capable of that. They can just split the time up until we get there. Even shifts. If there's, say, three more guys that are experienced enough to hold the wheel, then we'll just split it two-and-a-half-hour watches, or something like that. By the morning the captain will be up anyway.

Phil Torres

"

Kenny Santos mending a net.

"

Monking, we do pretty long tows that are like four or five hours sometimes. So, you can turn in, get some more sleep, you're pretty much just waiting for the net to come. You know, that time to go. Usually there's a couple people up at all times in case something happens. So, you have some people up if you have to haul the gear. Always have to have two people. One guy up in the wheelhouse and then one guy running the winches down on deck. So, usually try and keep two people up, at least. A lot of time is consumed waiting, you know? When it's nice like this, we spend some time up on the bow, catch some sun, look for sharks, whatever. Things to pass the time.

The captain and I, last monking trip, we were just working six hours on and six hours off. We were doing five- and six-hour tows, so we were just doing like one tow apiece. He'd do a tow and then I'd do a tow. And it would work like six hours. And then the guys on deck were running like every tow off between them. One guy would have a tow off in the bunk, between those. So, we'd always have three guys up, be able to handle the gear, and whatnot.

Usually start the winches back. Monking, there's a lot of wire. You're fishing in 200 fathom [1,200 feet], or deeper, so you have a lot of tow wire that needs to come back. And usually takes at least ten minutes to just haul the wire back. The wire comes up, doors come up on the end of the wire; it's what spreads the net. Hook the doors up and detach the net itself from the doors and hook it onto the net reel. And the net all comes up, haul that in, when the bag comes up, the guy in the wheelhouse takes it out of gear and goes down and runs the controls to bring the bag in. Bag's full of the fish. Bring the bag in, pop the bag in the pen where it goes. You can sort it all out. And you set it right back out again, hopefully, without any damage. Every tow you have to look at the net, make sure there's no damage. Really check it.

If things go smoothly, from the time that you start hauling the net, start hauling the doors and all the ground wire, until the time you set out and all the wire's out and the brakes are locked up is usually about 45 minutes. That's how long it takes a whole haul and set out in the deep water monking. Because there's a lot of wire and that just takes a long time no matter what, hauling or setting.

Phil Torres

"

Walter Allyn inside wheelhouse.

"

Sometimes when we get a foul set, or something where the doors cross over, or something happens where the gear rolls over itself, that can create situations. You have to really be on your toes and really know what you're doing to get it unwound or unknotted.

Phil Torres

Well, the newer boats today, you work with a net reel. Everything's done right over the stern. So when you're setting out, you're going straight ahead and everything's just straight off. You know, you just set right straight ahead. The net winds off the reel. With the newer boats everything's done right off the stern, through a ramp. Ramp built right into the stern of the boat. We use what we call split winches. You've got one on the port side and one on the starboard side. They're done hydraulically. You've got a pump down, running off the main engine, hydraulic pump. You've got two of them, one for each side. And you can adjust 'em right out there. You've got a hauling station where you just throw a lever and a guy can slow one down, speed one up. Normally when you're hauling there, you just snap 'em in right, wide open and let them rip. And they'll come together.

Unless of course you got something hung on one door, you know. An obstruction, a hang, whatever. And then you've got to work on it a little bit, tow it around, pull it up. But they come, we get 'em. You hang up and you'll be towing along and all of a sudden you'll feel her. She'll stop and you'll feel everything will start gurgling away at her motors, laboring and all of that. You know you're hung down. What you do immediately is just start the winches back, try to get the doors up as soon as you possibly can. Get them up and most of the time it will come right off the hang. You know, you get it straight up and down, once you get all the slack out of all the wires and stuff, and you get everything right straight up and down, the boat will go up on a sea or something and most of the time she'll come clear.

Jim Allyn

"

Winter at the dock.

"

You never throw the boat out of gear, always keep the boat in gear. Always. What will happen is you'll haul the wires back and the doors will come up and all you've got left then is your ground tackle. Now, if you're fishing in deep, deep water–say you're fishing a 100 fathoms of water and you've got 50 fathoms of ground gear out–then you're already clear. Where if you were fishing say in 30 fathoms and you've got 50 fathoms of ground gear out, after the doors come up and you disconnect and you put your ground wire on–and all your ground wire now goes on your net reel on a newer boats–what you'd have to do is just keep hauling it back until it either comes clear or you get it right straight up and down. And then you just kind of wait and work at it, hope for the best. But if you've got something heavy, usually you're gonna be all ripped up and busted up and you know you've got a lot of work ahead of you then.

Rocks, old wrecks, old wrecks. Most of the hangs now we pretty much got them located, you know, inshore out to say 50 fathoms. Like I've been monk-fishing there in the deep water out to 300 fathoms. We've been catching monkfish out there and we still occasionally find a new one out there, you know, and usually it's a big rock. Big rock, or a lot of it's government stuff too. They do a lot of dumping out there. You got a lot of government old bombs, and torpedoes, and what have you. You know, dummies.

Jim Allyn

Usually, you'll sense a lack of movement in the doors. When you try to set out, the doors will spread out, you'll see that in the wire. And if it's a foul set it will be right in close and you'll know it there. Or the speed of the boat. Say you set all your wire out, and you didn't know you foul set yet, then you'll notice it. After a few minutes the speed of the boat comes down to three knots or something. You'll know; you can feel how it's supposed to be. Also, you'll be going three and a half knots, you'll know that's not right; should be going real easy. So you have to haul, and you know it's a foul set. It doesn't happen often, but it has happened a few times out in the deep water. It's kind of like uncharted grounds out there.

Usually you take everything up on one side. You have the two wires going out and the two doors. Usually you'll just bring everything and it will come up on one door. So, you see what you need to do. It's just a matter of disconnecting things and taking the knot out, basically what it amounts to.

Phil Torres

"

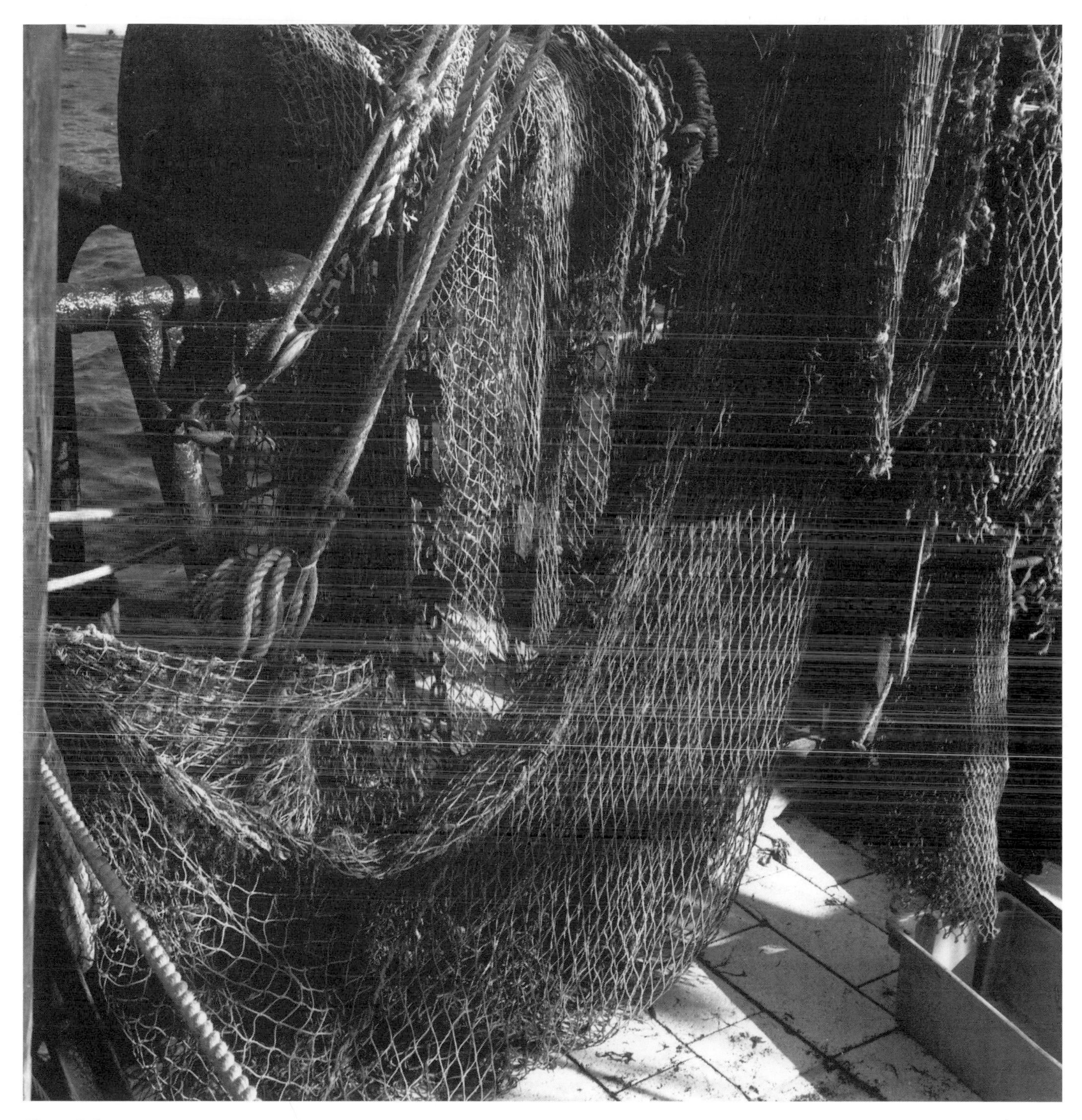

Net on deck.

"

In the hold of each boat, they have what they call pens. And it's blocked off into sections, pens. You can put one type of fish in one pen or another type in another pen, or different sizes in each pen. So, you can keep them sorted down in the fish hold. And you put like say two feet of ice on the bottom, just ice itself, and then you'll throw say five baskets of fish on, and ice that real good. And then the next tow's fish will go on top of that. Keep icing it as well. Well, ice is pretty much the least expensive thing on the expense list, so we never lack on the ice. We always make sure we have a lot of ice. Plus, our fish hold is very well insulated. So, it stays nice and cool even in the summer. Usually there's one guy on the boat, the hold man, who's pretty much in charge of everything down there. If something goes wrong down there, then it's his responsibility. So he pretty much stays on top of everything, makes sure everything's iced, everything looks good down there.

Our boat usually always fishes around the clock. Just about every single trip. The only time we do stop when we fish is during real bad weather in the wintertime, when you have to lay the boat up. But there's a lot of boats that go out and don't fish nights, say, because they don't think it's worth their while or whatever, but we don't stop. We just fish right around the clock. All the time.

Phil Torres

I've got a bunch of guys that are really working for you and they aren't trying to figure how to get out of something rather than just doing it. You know, you don't have to baby-sit; they know what they've got to do. They want to make money just as bad as you, that's what we're there for. We all work together and you get a good team. You get a good crew together, you don't have problems. Takes a long time though to get a good crew together. Takes a long time unless you're a real high-liner. But you've still got to weed 'em out. You still got a lot of weeding to do. Where, like a New Bedford boat, a lot of the crews, guys don't even know each other. Every trip's a different crew, a different crew. I couldn't fish like that. I wouldn't like it.

Jim Allyn

"

Trawl net.

"

We've got a TV, VCR. Lot of times you don't get any TV [reception], but we've got two VCRs now. You bring the tapes. Got a deal worked out with the tape shop down here. They give you $2.00 a movie. Keep it for as long as you want. So we get a movie a day, eight, nine movies, ten movies. A movie a day. You get off, you eat your dinner, you plug a movie in. You're watching a movie while you're eating. Might stay up another hour or so. Hour and a half, watch half of it, something like that. We don't play much cards. I guess a lot of boats might plays cards and stuff like that. The guys like to read a lot. Read in your bunk. Get a good book. After a hard watch, get comfortable, get in your bunk and read a book. You get tired. Next thing you know, you're out. Somebody's shaking you, time to get up again. That's about it. We sit up on the bow in the nice weather, you know. You get a nice lawn chair, kick back in between tows, when there isn't anything going on. You learn to pass the time.

No alcohol. No alcohol on the boat at all. Absolutely not. Just doesn't mix. Alcohol and water don't mix at all. No. Once in a while you let them take a six-pack for the ride home or something, you know. Have a beer apiece, ride home after working. Once in a while, you know. If they have a steak night or something, you let them have a beer or something. Not too often though. They don't even want it, you know. They get enough of it when they get ashore. They're good guys.

We eat very well. Very, very well. We've always had a good cook on my boat. Won't go without one. We'll eat anything, from chicken to turkey. We have a big turkey dinner once a trip, on the longer trips. Big steak dinner, fresh salads, fruits in the morning. It's all sliced up. The cook, that's his job, you know.

Jim Allyn

"

Michael Medeiros in fish hold.

"

What we do is eat twice a day. We'll have a breakfast, generally cook breakfast at six, seven o'clock in the morning. What you try to do is, the cook has the breakfast ready when the watch shifts. So if the watch is shifting at say eight, we'll eat at eight. You know, it depends on when you start your watch, when the trip begins really. Could be six, could be seven, could be eight. Either that or they'll come off deck, sit down, grab something quick, if they don't feel like eating when they first get up. That was a problem with me. You get out of the bunk, you know, the last thing you want to do is sit down, eat a turkey dinner. Right fresh out of bed, you know. So you go out on deck for an hour or so. You just make a plate up; we've got microwaves.

Jim Allyn

The first day, and on the way out, we're not really worried about it. We end up setting around seven. Usually when we set out for the first day, everybody's up and everybody's ready to set out, so we all set out and the cook will just go in and make us something to eat for breakfast while we're setting out and he'll have it ready for us when we get off deck. We usually run a shift where the cook is up at certain times of the day when you want to eat. Eat at six o'clock or something in the morning.

You can snack any time you want. One thing we don't slack on is food. Always eat pretty good on our boat. We usually have a cook, cooks us breakfast and dinner every day, and [the boat carries] plenty of stuff to eat other than that in between. Always coffee; there's always a pot of coffee made, with a machine that makes it in two and a half minutes, something like that. Coffee's a big priority on the boat. We could have anything from blueberry pancakes to fried dough or omelettes, you know, whatever. Every day it's something different, sausage, eggs. Can have anything from fettucini Alfredo primavera to pot roast or calzones. We eat very good. All boneless food. Couple trips ago we were getting filet mignons. We got our steak night, rib-eye steaks or something. Boneless pork and whatnot. We eat pretty good.

Phil Torres

"

Scallop Boat Routine

Bags of scallops.

Scallop boats are comparable in size to the offshore draggers, running up to 100 feet in length. They usually carry an even number of crew members, with six men being a common number. Trips typically last ten days or more. The men fish around the clock, often in eight-hour shifts. They work at a fast pace, hauling two specially designed dredges in tows that last less than an hour. A mate on a scallop boat, as well as an offshore dragger, may have extended responsibility, supervising one of the shifts or watches. Since scallops are shellfish, onboard processing differs from the routine on draggers. The scallops are removed from their shells, or shucked, before they are iced or flash-frozen. When off watch, the men occupy themselves in the same manner as the crews of the offshore draggers, by sleeping, eating, or relaxing with magazines or videos.

"When we're scalloping we run five days in, twelve days out.

Walter Allyn

Well, scalloping, we'll run like 18-hour steam; we've got an 18-hour run out of Stonington. And what we generally try to do is run a shift. Some guys go six hours on, six hours off. You've got two shifts. This guy goes six on, they go off, this crew comes on for six, and you make up a 24-hour day like that. We go eight and eight on our boat. My boat, the guys kind of like the eight and eight better. They'd rather do the extra two hours on deck and then get the extra two hours off because they're long trips and you need your rest. If we're six-handed, there'd be three down and three up.

Jim Allyn

Scalloping is a whole different routine, it's a whole different pace. You leave the dock, you know you're leaving for 10 or 11 days at least. The boat is totally full of fuel, as much as it can hold. We've put an extra 500 gallon tank on it, just so we could get another day out there. You don't use nets, or doors. You use dredges. Big 13- or 15-foot dredges that ride right along the bottom. You use two of those. And you work eight hours on and eight hours off. Scalloping you need more men to run both shifts 24 hours a day. So, you usually take an even amount; say, six guys. Three on one watch and three on another watch. So, you work eight hours on and eight hours off, rotating with the other watch. That's about it. I run one watch and the captain runs the other watch.

You set them both in the water at the same time and you usually tow them from 40 to 50 minutes. Every 50 minutes they're coming back, so the pace is totally different, from five hours [dragging] to every 40 minutes [scalloping]. You know, always whoosh, whoosh, bringing the wire in and out, always setting. Usually when you're working scallops there's a whole fleet of boats around also. So, you're working with the other guys and you're always working in the same area, scalloping.

Usually it just skims the bottom. You don't really want it to dig too much or else you'll get too much stuff in the dredge itself. Sometimes you get too much and you can't lift it. Sometimes you work right in the rocks yourself. Scallops like the rocks, and a lot of the times every tow you'll be working right in the rocks where you have to literally pick boulders up and throw them over every trip. I've been on trips that I've seen enough rocks to easily fill this house a couple times in one trip, you know? That's how many rocks you literally shove over, kick over the boat every 40 minutes. So, in the course of a trip, you could easily fill this house with rocks. It's tough work when you're working in the rocks, that's for sure."

Phil Torres

Taking out scallops.

"

The two dredges will come up at the same time or come up to the blocks on each side of the boat, and you have a three-man shift, so when they come up, the captain or me, who's running the boat, will throw it out of gear, run down, and run the controls. There's two hooks on each side of the two booms on the boat to work each dredge. So, you bring both dredges right in with the steel chain bags and drop them right on deck. And they're made to dump a certain way. You know, they're built so you can dump them on the boat. Then you dump them and you throw one part back over, you take the hook out, you put it right back into the dredge itself, and then, boom, drop the dredge right back over. Take it up back into the block and set out. Soon as you put it back into gear, and you turn around and you get the boat going the way you want it, the guys in the back will plane them out. There's a chain back there for it. And you put the chain on it, and you let the dredge out a little bit on the winch, and it planes it out so they're planing nice and flat and even in the back. And you get going the way you want to go, and they set them right out. Sometimes you'll get them and they'll flop over like that on the way down, back drop, you know. You won't get anything in that one.

Like, say, you're supposed to set them as the boat rolls on the down roll. You're supposed to set that one like that. Sometimes if you set them too fast or something, the tide's going the wrong way, bunch of variables involved, you may get one that drops over and gets a back drop or something. Or if you turn the boat while you're setting. Sometimes you'll just get them and they ride each other, because it's not really too far apart, but you know, sometimes they'll ride each other and you won't get too much in one, but you'll get them in the other one. When you're working for that eight-hour shift and trying to get as many bags, it can be frustrating if you get a couple like that in a row, you know. Your whole watch is gone. You can't make up the bags that you wanted to make up. It's tough right now. It's tough business right now, scalloping.

Process is, you throw the baskets out in each corner of the pile and start picking through the pile, and putting all the scallops into the baskets. And throwing and kicking all the stuff out the scupper holes in the sides of the boats that you don't use. Usually there's three guys doing that. So, after that, you're all done cleaning the deck, cleaning all the stuff off the deck, you take the baskets and you bring them up forward, and up forward, underneath the upper deck, there's a place to process the scallops. Shucking boxes. So, you dump all the scallops in the shucking boxes, and you have your bucket and your knife, and you shuck all the scallops there. The guys on deck do most of the shucking.

Phil Torres

"

Scallop dredge.

"

At the end of your eight-hour shift or six-hour shift, you bag them up while the other shift is coming on deck, so there's no downtime. They come on, and then you stop, and then you start to back up. You put them all in a huge garbage bucket during your eight hours, and at the end of your eight hours you take them out and you put them in like a perforated bin, big sieve-type thing. And you rinse them all out, and you have to count them all up. You take counts per pound. There's no count now, but there used to be. You had to have them within 33 or 36 individual scallops per pound. But now they've done away with that. But you still end up counting them, because now there's different prices for the different counts. Like, say, 10-20, you'll get $6.50 [per pound] for it. Those are big scallops.

So, then you go to 20-30, and the price will drop a little bit. You get up into 50-, 60-, 70-count stuff, it's really tiny stuff and they can't really do too much with that, so the price is less. You only get like $3.00 [per pound] for that stuff. Usually, probably around 42 pounds per bag. We usually call it 42. And it usually comes out a little bit more. It's almost like cheese-cloth, but tighter woven. You want them to breathe, because as soon as you put scallops in an unbreathable bag, the bacteria starts growing in them; as soon as you put them in a sealed bag. So, you put them in bags, and you put the bags down in each pen in the fish hold. You stack the bags side by side, and you don't let them touch each other. You put ice between them, and then you make another row on top of that when you're done with that row.

Usually you know, you have the 42 pound average. We call one of our bags 42 pounds. So, at the end of the trip, if we had a hundred bags, we know we got about 4,200 pounds, at least. So, when you come out you may get one that's 46 or you might get one that's 41. The average usually works out to about 42, 43. So, we tell them over the radio how much we think we have, and as we're taking the bags out they weigh each bag. That's critical on scallops, too.

These days it works out better if you individualize them; you know, if you separate them into your different counts. So, you put them in different pens down in the fish hold. You know which ones are which. Like that's the 60-count stuff over there, and some 20-count stuff over here. And you get better money for them that way.

Phil Torres

"

Weighing scallops at dock.

"

We work around the clock for 11 days, until you're out of fuel. Our boat holds 6,850 gallons of fuel. So, we usually burn around 550 gallons a day. It's usually anywhere between 60 and 80 cents. Right around there, 70 cents. It's not too bad. A few years it was pretty bad when the fuel prices were up. So, we only get about 10, 11 days in. And it's still another 12 hours to get back to home.

You either sleep or you hang out up in the wheelhouse, or you watch a movie or read a book. We always get magazines and we got a big stack of magazines and newspapers and stuff, every time we go food shopping, to keep us busy. If there's work to be done on the gear, between tows we'll work on the gear. When you're scalloping there's usually a day right in the middle of the trip where you take a couple hours and you go through your gear and spruce it up, so to say, a little bit. There's cards, there's backgammon. We're not too big on cards on our boat. We haven't really played too much cards. Keep busy with your crossword puzzles or whatnot.

Well, the expenses.... You get a trip of, say, $30,000 or so, the expenses come off the top: fuel, ice, grub. The business, I believe, gets 53 percent, and the boat itself gets 40. The crew gets the 47 percent. We share it up that way.

Phil Torres

On some of these scallop trips when we have a large crew, the food bill can be anywhere from $1,500 to $2,000. That's for twelve days.

Walter Allyn

"

Navigation, Weather, and the Seasons

Joe Kessler's finger.

Two factors greatly influence the process of getting to, and safely and comfortably working on, the fishing and lobstering grounds navigation and weather. Today's fishermen have vast advantages over their predecessors in their ability to navigate. Radar, loran, sounding devices, and other equipment provide highly detailed information about the position of the boat and the depth and nature of the ocean bottom. Cellular phones and radios provide easy access to updat ed weather information.

Weather is a fishermen's greatest adversary. Fishermen and lobstermen work every month of the year, but the weather often limits their work. Poor conditions can keep boats at the dock. Rapid changes may create dangerous conditions, forcing a hasty return to port. Electronic navigation gear is a great aid in many conditions, such as fog, but it provides no defense from the sometimes battering effects of the wind and elements.

Seasonal changes are accompanied by prolonged and dramatic weather variations; most notably, temperature shifts. But fishermen give less concern to temperature than they do another, more critical weather factor: the wind. The winter usually brings heavy winds–usually cold and dry from the northwest or wet and stormy from the northeast–which may create dangerously high seas, both inshore and offshore. Working on deck in strong winds and breaking seas is difficult and dangerous. Winds can also blow freezing spray, icing a vessel and making her dangerously top-heavy. Technology provides many advantages, but weather is always a force to be reckoned with.

"

To compare the old style to the new style, the navigational aids they have today, it's the state of the art. These guys can stay on their tow within 20 feet. It's no problem. They got the whole ocean floor charted. They know where every obstruction is. Information is passed from one to the other, so you get a repertoire that's real big.

The navigational aids; God, they carry two of everything: two radars, two lorans, three or four sounding machines, four or five telephones, chromoscopes, electronic plotters that work off the lorans. It's really something, and they're very good at what they do with it. For one of us old-timers to go in there and start pushing buttons, you might as well close the door because we're not computer-oriented. These young fellows that grew up with computers, it's very simple to them. And they're very good.

Walter Allyn

That was a great thing when they put direction finders aboard boats. Radios and direction finders. You talk about a revelation. They came up with a sounding machine; an electronic sounding machine that told you how deep the water was. Wow, what a difference that made. We used to have to throw a lead line overboard to get a depth. Especially in foggy weather, when you're making a beach or coming in and the weather was bad, your first landfall was most important, because from there the skipper knew where he was. And he could, using a clock and a compass, could get himself anywhere.

Something we don't do today: we depend on electronics, and we don't do it on course and time. For instance, I could tell you from memory that from the Watch Hill buoy to the Napatree Point buoy, you steered west-by-north-a-half-north for nine minutes in my father's old boat. And when you did nine minutes, you stopped the boat and listened for the bell. See? And you'd get that far and then you'd make a course for Stonington breakwater and listen for the bell. If the bell didn't ring, we'd run around in circles for a little while, make enough rough water for the bell to ring. And then we'd know where the bell was. Things like this, this is what they used.

And, of course, lorans and navigation equipment came one right after the other. I can remember in 1956, when I asked my father to buy a radar, and he said, "What the hell is a radar?" He says, "What do you mean things that you can't see?" And we bought a Bendix radar. He was completely amazed. He didn't ever use it; he was already ashore, we had turned him ashore. But he was completely amazed that you had something that you could see in the nighttime, in the fog, and in the dark, where you didn't have to go up and make these buoys. But that's the way things evolved in the fishing business. It came slow, but it came steady, you know?

"

Joe Rendeiro

Miss Karyn through *Seafarer*'s rigging.

"

We get a lot of fog, so you have to be pretty knowledgeable with the radar and that kind of thing because all our gear's set on loran lines. Years ago, when I didn't have a radar on my other boats and didn't have a loran to speak of –had A loran; now we've got C–couldn't haul in the fog. Stuff wasn't on loran lines. I remember one year I was in 20-something days straight because we had fog every day; didn't clear off until four o'clock in the afternoon. Well, now it's get up at quarter after three, I'm at the dock by about ten of four, and we're leaving whether you can see your hand in front of your face or whether it's crystal clear; we're going.

You get the confidence of learning. I mean, the first few times with the radar I was a little nervous. It was like you didn't want to screw up and end up on Watch Hill, you know, or on the reef. But once you build your confidence up with using the equipment and knowing where you're going, it's no different than an airplane pilot.

Mike Grimshaw

We've got single-sideband radios now that they never had in the old days. We can generally talk just about anywhere we want with these things. They're an AM-band radio, and we get a weather report at six and twelve in the morning and at night. Comes out of Newport News, a high seas report. Or you can get one right out of Boston. That comes out at 5:40 and at 11:40. You tune in on a channel there and you get a weather report. You kind of make your decision there, what you're going to do. I've got a barometer, that comes in. You take what this guy's got to say for the weather. He gives it 20 to 30 or a 30 to 40 [knot wind] or whatever, and you kind of go with your barometer and look the situation over and use your best judgment from there, whether you're going to be able to fish or not.

Jim Allyn

Some boats now have a weather fax machine built right in. So, if they want the weather, they just punch in what they want and it'll come out on a read out. They have all the isobars, and they can pretty much make their own judgment of what it's going to be through that. We don't have that yet.

You usually rely on what they tell you. We look at the barometer a lot. We judge the weather a lot by our barometer, and usually things happen so fast that it's not a matter of looking out the window. It could be nice right now, and half hour from now a storm could come up. The easterly winds, they usually come up real fast, and you don't realize it until sometimes it's too late. And then, boom, you're in the middle of a storm. Summertime, you don't really monitor it that closely, but in the wintertime, even on land, you're monitoring the weather and where it is, where you're going to fish. Every day you'll go down, hear the weather, listen to the weather, our shore captain, the owner of the boat, Walter Allyn, has single sideband right at his house, so we can communicate back and forth there.

"

Phil Torres

Jim McPherson.

"

Now, they run around with these electronics; they see a school of fish, they set on the fish. Then, when you got the loran, that gave a little more. A little tool. With loran you can fish in the fog. All that because you can come in and out when you want to. Each thing made it easier.

George Berg

Snow doesn't keep us in. It's the wind. Wind, and if it's severely cold, we don't bother either. It's dangerous, the decks are all icy all the time and you take one little slip and "bye bye." But last winter, in all the years I've been doing it, financially, was just terrible. We didn't make a plug nickel. We couldn't get out. This year the weather has been a little bit better. Just a little.

Well, I had to go down and shovel the boat today. I wouldn't have had to if it didn't snow. You've got to worry about ice when you're out and it is cold and you're throwing the spray up. It can be disastrous if you don't stop and chop it off. The other night we came in with the snowstorm that started Tuesday. Most of the way in we knew we only had a couple of hours ride, so it wasn't getting too critical. But when I got outside of Watch Hill and the reefs and everything, I wanted to make sure I was going through the right places. I got out and chopped ice off my windows. It was an inch and a half thick.

Things freeze. Your deck hoses, you've got to drain them at night, and you have to make sure your engines are kept warm and put antifreeze in them. If all that isn't kept up and you go down the next morning, and you turn the key–just like if your automobile is frozen solid–you're not going to go anywhere. There is a lot to it.

Tim Medeiros

Well, in my opinion, the winter's the worst time. We're fishing on the continental shelf for the most part. You get bad weather from the east, or normally where it'll come from, northeast, east, southeast. It's always backed up with a vicious nor'wester, which beats you to death one way and turn around and do it again the other; where in the summertime, the winds are softer. They don't have the weight, they don't seem to be as heavy, don't kick the sea up like it does in the winter. You can take about anything comes along in the summer. Wintertime you get beat up pretty good.

Walter Allyn

"

Taking out in winter.

"Thirty-five in the summer is nothing. They get that, it's very common. Twenty-five, thirty practically every day offshore. You get your flat days, too. Depending, of course, where you are. And then, of course, you've got to remember one thing: weather's only part of it. If you're fishing up this way, what we call the southern fishing, south of Block Island and on the continental shelf and areas like that, Hudson Canyon, Tom's Canyon, you're in a relatively protected place. The tide doesn't run like it does east. You can get a lot of wind and fish a lot of wind there without any problem. Where you take the same breeze, go east down on Georges, fight the rips and where you got a tremendous tide on the northern edge, southeast part, sou'west part. Cultivator [Shoal], tide seems to smoke real hard there, this channel. The weather could be lighter, but the sea conditions would be much worse. So yes, weather's got a lot to do with it, but so has the place you're at.

Walter Allyn

If you're way down east and you might want to beat it back to the west eight to ten hours or so. Get a little closer just in case you do get a big breeze. You definitely get some big breezes in the wintertime. But, like I say, you get caught in a breeze, you know, you just get the deck secured, tie everything down. Just let the boat take care of itself. Hold her up into the wind there; keep a guy up all the time keeping an eye on things and generally you don't have no problems. Only problems are the ones you create, you're creating yourself. Pushing 'em. A lot of times a guy pushes 'em too hard. You're trying to get back; thinks he's gonna get under cover or something, and that doesn't cut it. You've got to let it go nice and easy, slow. In bad weather, just let the boat take care of herself; just let her go easy. Jog. She'll take care of it. Just jog along, hold your ground or whatever.

You've got to use good judgment, you know. If you feel the boat isn't handling the weather good then you hold her up into the seas more or something. Angle it different. Tack a little bit, like the old schooners did. Usually, generally, you get 10, 12, 14, 15, 18 hours in a northeaster and she'll let go. That's all you're looking at; 12 hours southeast weather, she'll start letting go. You're gonna shift anyway. You're gonna get a wind shift, 12 hours in a southeaster. Northeaster you usually go 18 hours. You're gonna get a wind shift; gonna swing around to the north usually. In the wintertime they're swinging around up into the north and you get the big nor'west behind it. The cold air after the storm; where, in the spring, in the fall, you get the southeasters. Weather will swing into the southern and you get the sou'west behind that and warmer air.

Jim Allyn"

Mike Grimshaw hauling.

"

Those nor'westers, oh, they're bastards. Boy, them nor'westers, they're colder than hell. They ice up, make a lot of ice. That's what you've got to be careful of. Ice, that's the worst. You've got to make sure your vessel isn't icing up, you know. You get heavier up on the top, get rolling deep, and no good. You've got to stop, break it all off, shovel it overboard. These will flop on you, these stern trawlers. These steel boats, they will flop.

Jim Allyn

When I think about the winter, I think about wind. And I think about the summer, and I don't think about wind. Basically, in the wintertime, there's always a sea on, there's always wind going. That's when you really have to keep an eye on the weather. In summertime, we hardly even listen to the weather. We can usually fish all the time in the summertime. The wintertime you really have to keep on the weather and fish between bad storms. Sometimes you get caught out there in a storm and you have to lay through the storm. It's not worth your while to come in for the storm and have to come all the way right back out. There's really just calm in the summer and the fall. Sometimes it can start kicking up in October; November is a bad month; January is a bad month; and March sometimes can be real bad for weather. This last, past winter we had some real bad weather which consumed a lot of time. Fortunately, we were pretty much on the schedule where it ended up between the storms. And we were home anyway for them, but you know a lot of guys lose money because they have to come in for the storms. So, we did pretty good last winter with the storms.

Phil Torres

Yes, in a winter gale it probably could be rain and sleet and snow all at once. Usually it's raining sideways because the wind is blowing so much. You can hear the rigging "freight training," we call it. It's just noisy air. Usually you lay up for however long it takes to pass: 12 hours sometimes, a day sometimes. And you just jog pretty much on idle right into the sea. And it's usually the smoothest ride. So you're not going real fast, and you're not really bucking it, pounding, or anything. You're just kind of, almost, sitting in the same spot, just going right into it. Usually, if we're laying, there's got to be at least 30- or 40-foot seas going. If we're laying to. Usually; it kind of depends. It all depends on the situation at the time. But usually 15-, 20-foot seas, we're still fishing. Scalloping's a little bit different because the gears can get a little wild. Scalloping you really have to watch out and be careful. There's a lot of safety factors involved–personal safety–scalloping. So, we're real careful not to fish too much in bad weather in the wintertime. Some guys fish right through it and they never stop, and you know, sometimes it's crazy, but that's the way it is.

Phil Torres

"

Taking out at Sea-Rich.

"

[Lobstering], you know, 20 knots, 30 knots, you can get away with playing around inside if you've got some lees to work with. During the summertime we never take a day off unless it's going to be like 25- or 30-knot winds. And we only run into that situation towards the end of August. If it's below that and workable, we'll go out there and we'll try it. Maybe we want to haul 600, maybe we can only get 400 of them. Instead of being done at two o'clock in the afternoon, maybe heading for home, we may not be done until four o'clock.

Mike Grimshaw

I've run into a lot of people who said, "Well, you don't go out in the winter, do you?" And I see the shock and disbelief in John Rita's face and my father's face, "Of course, you do. There are some days you can't get out because it's too windy." "But," they said, "doesn't it get cold out there?" And they don't really understand what you go through. Most people, whether it be a powerboat or a sailboat, they go out, they pick the nice days in the summer. And they don't understand that the sea goes to the other extreme also, and that fishermen have to go out either way. Whenever you can, you do. And if it's raining, you get wet.

Michael Medeiros

Last winter was really tough. You always prepare for the worst winters, and if you can prepare yourself before, you won't have any problems. You can go two, three weeks without being out one day. Last winter, we counted the days. In February they might have gone out four or five days out of the whole month.

Ann Rita

You have to respect the weather and respect what it can do. My father says there are three ages of fishing: there's 20, 40, and 60. And at the age of 20, you make a lot of bad decisions, especially if you're running a boat. My father said he went out in weather that he had no business going out in. And then, by the time you're 40, you've had enough close calls to really be cautious about it and gain the respect that you need–if you've lived that long and stayed in the business that long. And then, he said, at 60, sometimes you've seen too much, and you see how quickly storms can form, and how violent things can get. And sometimes you're a little bit too cautious toward the end of your career. He said it happened to a point with him, and he saw it happening with other older fishermen.

Michael Medeiros

"

Dock Work and Shoreside Activity

Net-mending gear.

The fishermen's work doesn't end when he offloads his catch. With their boats secured at their berths, there is often additional work to be done. Maintenance and other dockside work is a constant, year-round responsibility. Lobstermen work at the time-consuming task of stringing bait. Captains and crewmembers of draggers and scallopers mend and repair nets and dredges. Other gear may require maintenance, or electronic equipment may have to be installed. To save money, the men do much of this work themselves. Good mechanical skills are valuable in this line of work.

Seasonal projects also demand attention. Boats are usually hauled once a year. Major projects, such as engine replacement or hull work, are generally scheduled during slow seasons such as winter so valuable time isn't lost during peak fishing periods. Lobstermen use their slower seasons to build new pots, repair old ones, or knit new funnels.

"

Fishermen are a close-knit group, too, regardless of their ethnic background. They still are a very proud, close-knit group. And when an emergency arises, they're all there. That's what our association in Stonington, right now, is all about. It's a bonding together of several people in the same profession to try to have the best things done for us and to do the best things that we can do. That's it in a nutshell. We're very close, we're very proud, and we don't like to be trod on. We're independent.

Walter Allyn

There is always something to do. Whether it be net repair, or you have an oil change. There is always something: ground gear, something could be measured. We tend to let things go, especially in the good weather, because if you are making money you just keep going, keep going, keep going. And you end up with a list of things that long, and when you do get a day off you get maybe half of them done. The rest of them grow, and then you get some more. If you go down and look at my boat right now, maybe to you it might look good, but I could point out about 50 things on it that have to be done–that should have been done a long time ago–and they're not, and you can't do them in this kind of weather, either.

[Tourists or visitors] come to the dock a lot of times. Some [fishermen] won't even bother with them. I like to come in, throw the lines on the dock, and go home. But especially in the summer those people are all up and down the docks with their little bags, a couple of bucks sticking out of their pocket [hoping to buy fish]. It's comical sometimes, but other times it gets under your skin. They just stand there, usually with their hands out looking for bargains. Sorry to say, they don't get them many times, and they wonder why. "Come on, give me a deal," and I'll be standing there thinking, "You want a deal from me? Do you know what I've been through all day long?" They just want a bargain. They're not happy a lot of times, and I don't think they realize what we have to go through. Maybe they just don't give a darn.

Tim Medeiros

"

Arthur Medeiros mending.

Al Maderia (L) and John DeBragga.

The Boats

Sternboard, *Susan & Frances*.

The boats of the Stonington fleet range in length from about 25 feet to 80 feet, and all are powered by diesel engines. The boats are central to the fishermen's work, and so they are given careful attention. Some fishermen feel an especially strong bond with their boats, to a degree that may be difficult for those outside the fishing community to appreciate. A fisherman's boat functions as the primary tool of his livelihood. It also provides him with transportation to and from work, and it protects him from the elements–which is very important when you consider where he works. In a sense, the fisherman's boat almost seem to be a member of his family. They are usually named after wives, daughters, mothers, or other female family members. Even if he is not going out on the water, the fisherman or lobsterman goes down to the dock and checks his boat every day. They are checked after snowstorms, on Christmas, and on other holidays. The loss of a boat due to sale or sinking is a demoralizing experience for a fisherman, and for his family members who understand how much it means to him, and to them.

"

Today, some of these boats, these 90-footers, have 1,240 horsepower. One of them 1,500 horsepower.

Al Maderia

And now, we find ourselves in the *Matthew Melissa*, which is 76 feet, 775 horse, steel, built in Panama City, Florida. My oldest son's is 80 feet. She's got 960-horse Caterpillar [engine], and she was built in Houma, Louisiana, by Maine Iron Works. She's relatively new: three years.

Walter Allyn

Now I've got the *Matthew Melissa*. She's 76 foot. Stern trawler. And what we did was we rigged her up for scalloping, right away. Replated all the decks, extra plate, boxed all the rails in with steel plate and all of that stuff. And then we put a new engine in her. Went from a 12-92, that's 92 cubic inches cylinder, 12 cylinders; that's about a 500-horse engine. And what we did was repowered it with a 12-149. That's a big engine. A 149 cubic inch and I'm up to like 700 horse there now. I'm co-owner, captain, and I've been running her for five years. Pretty good rig. Yeah, she treats me good. Good boat.

All the stabilizers really do is make it comfortable. The boats all get a stability test. They're all done without the outriggers. Whenever you do a stability test on a boat, no outriggers, your outriggers are up. So they're generally just there for the comfort, you know. And boy they do help, believe me. Set those big wings down and then we drop what we call a bird off of them, they hang off the end, it's like a big flat triangle piece. And that hangs down in the water, 30, 40 feet on chain right from the end of the outrigger and they just slow the roll right down, you know. They take that snap out of stuff. Makes it a lot more comfortable. They do. They work good.

Jim Allyn

Yeah, well, nowadays maintenance on a boat requires sandblasting and things of that nature, and spray painting, and we don't have the equipment for it or a place to do it or anything else.
Not like the old days. The old days we had all the time in the world to do it. Nowadays, downtime is money. We want that boat at sea as quick as we can get her there. So consequently, in the long run it's just as cheap to hire it done as it is tying the boat up for a longer period of time. That's the way we do it.

Walter Allyn

"

Boats at dock.

"

Well, you've got to haul them. You've got to haul them every two years, at least. You've got to re-zinc the bottom and paint them up and change the bearing on the propellers where the shaft comes through. You've got to do all that. Right now they're sandblasting. She got a little chewed up there, around the stern, so they're doing a little sandblasting. And they put a three-coat system on, paint. I've got my propeller off; that's getting all reconditioned. My rudder had a bad bearing in it; that's getting a new bearing in it. It was all sloppy back there, getting ready to fall off. So, it's been two years since I hauled the boat. So, I sent her to get a little loving. Little tender loving care. We all need it. I'm looking at a $23,000 bill. Twenty-three thousand. That's what the contract read. So it isn't cheap. Big business today, you know.

Jim Allyn

I think right now it's too much of a liability to own a boat, as far as a new buyer would be concerned, because if you don't have the right boat, and you don't have the versatility in your boat–some of these boats don't have the versatility we have; we can be scalloping one day, and monking the next day, and fluking the next day, and swill fishing the next day if we wanted to–you know, they don't have the versatility in their boat where it has enough power or it's heavy duty enough to handle scallop dredges or things like that. We've put a lot of investment, a lot of time and money into the boat to build it so it's tough enough to handle all the different things. It's rigged out to handle all the different types of fishing we want to do with it.

Phil Torres

The old days, people were more dedicated. The boat was their life. They took care of another man's property like it was their own. It's not that way today. Today, I think everything revolves around the dollar. They want to see how much they can make regardless of how much they take out of the equipment. A family-owned boat is not that way because the captain running the boat, he has to pay both bills. His personal bills plus the boat bill, you know, if he owns a piece of it. So, it makes a difference. Yes, it does.

Walter Allyn

Sundays I just say we're not doing anything. We get up, we go to church, and I go down to the boat, look at the lines, and make sure everything's fine and that will do it.

Tim Medeiros

That boat was his life, and as he says, the boat came first. The money was spent on the boat because that earned us our living. I understood that.

Doris Berg

"

The Dock

Matthew Melissa.

The Town Dock serves as the center of operations for the Stonington fleet. The local fishermen's group, the Southern New England Fishermen's and Lobstermen's Association, leases it from the town. The dock is managed and maintained by the association. The dock is actually "U"-shaped, with two long piers extending out into the water. Each of these has a number of berths for the fishing vessels. Two buildings on the north pier house fish buyers, an office for the fishermen's association, a dockmaster's office, and a meeting room. Loading docks at the rear of the buildings facilitate the shipping of fish by truck. Other facilities at the dock include two industrial-size ice machines and a distribution setup for fuel. There is also substantial space for vehicle parking.

A dockmaster, employed by the association, runs the dock and keeps track of the comings and goings of boats. He also distributes ice, fuel, and supplies. The ice is essential for keeping fish fresh, especially on longer trips. The present dockmaster is also a diver, and he is able to do hull inspections, for example, if there is a problem with a boat.

Once the boats return to the dock from their trips or day's work, many of them tie up temporarily in front to the facilities belonging to one of several buyers or fish wholesalers. These businesses lease their space from the Fishermen's Association. The fish are unloaded in a process referred to as "taking out." Severe catch restrictions in recent years have made this a fairly quick process for the day boats since they generally return with small quantities of fish. Once it has offloaded its daily catch, the boat moves to its designated berth at the dock.

"A guy named Longo owned the property and had a trucking company. And he also bought fish, trucked the fish to New York. He trucked other things, too. Well, the boats were here. Of course, there was no place for them to go, then. I don't think there was any stipulation in the sale, but I guess Longo was willing to sell it to the town kind of with the understanding that the fishermen still would be able to use it. I don't know if this was in writing, or what. But ever since the town bought it, they've leased it to the fishermen on a nominal lease, long-term basis. We're the Southern New England Fishermen's and Lobstermen's Association. They've got about 200 members, I guess. And we've done all the improvements.

The weather's our biggest killer. We're not protected. We've got the breakwaters, but from the southeast, or anything easterly, southeasterly, or westerly, there's no protection at all. You get a tremendous surge in here; you can't even take out if it's real bad. And we've been talking back and forth with the Corps of Engineers for a long time, and you know how slow those things are. So, we have very limited room.

The boats pay wharfage, and that goes into a wharfage account. Wharfage account is used strictly for dock maintenance and repair. And we also have a working account, which is profits we make from selling fuel and ice and oil and supplies; you know, all the stuff that I sell. We keep some of that in reserve, but most of that is used for maintaining the dock. Well, for instance, the ice machine cost $300,000. We're paying that off. We pay for the fuel tanks. We pay for the fuel pump.

We're paying for these buildings. We're still paying for this building. The town doesn't pay anything. We bought all the stuff, and if we were ever to dissolve of course we couldn't take it with us; it would revert to town ownership. They belong to us as long as we're here. But if we ever dissolve they revert to the town. In effect, we can't take any money out of this. Say if we have $50,000, I think that reverts to the town, too. So, it's basically a nonprofit. It's run as a business, but it's a business to maintain the dock so the fishing fleet has a place to function out of. There's more and more state-owned facilities for fishing boats because the commercial land has become so valuable. There's a boatbuilding company in Maine that had to quit building boats because they were on the water. They couldn't afford to build boats there. They had to sell it for condos. Point Judith, the closest big fishing fleet, that's state land. New Bedford, I think the town owns a lot of the waterfront there. Gloucester, they just put in a big, fancy, new state pier."

Dick Bardwell

Dick Bardwell in dockmaster's office.

"

The wharfage money is all spent for upkeep of the dock. And a large percentage of the working account–any money we make as profit–goes back into the dock. We also have gotten some federal grants. And we got a grant from Farm Credit, which I guess is federal government, too, to do the dredging. And we got another grant to do some dock repair here. Because, you know, when you're talking about pilings, you don't talk about hundreds of dollars, you talk about thousands of dollars.

Well, we have a board of directors, and a business manager. I'm the dockmaster. We kind of all work together. For major things, we hire an engineering firm. Can't do anything without the engineering firm, you know, for any kind of a major project, which is true any place, I guess.

For the last seven or eight years we've had some North Carolina boats who come up and work out of here in the summertime, for two or three months. We've had boats from Point Judith come and take out. We've had Montauk boats come and take out. We've had a few small boats from down the Sound come here for supplies or to take out fish. A lot of boats just come and take out. The boats that stay pay a nominal nightly fee, which is $6.00 a night, which doesn't mean anything, really.

We have two fish buyers paying rent for one thing. The whole purpose of the Association is the benefit the fishermen. That's all their equipment. We just rent the space, as far as the fish buyers go. We're paying for the building, we're paying the mortgage on the building, but their rent helps to pay the mortgage on the building. They own their own equipment that's inside the building.

As I say, we're not in the business to make money, other than for the individual fishermen to be able to make a living fishing. We're here to provide a service, and in order to keep the fish buyers in business, they've got to have product. And that's going to become tougher and tougher all the time, because there's less and less product. So, the more boats that come in, it's good for the dock because they buy fuel and ice. And we make a profit on that so we can turn around and put that back into the dock. There's a lot of dissension there. Somebody will say big boats coming in do more damage than they're worth–for what they put in–but there's always somebody with a negative attitude.

Dick Bardwell

"

Cutting fish, Stonington Fillet.

"

I say the more business the better, the more boats the better. It's good for everybody. It's good for the town, the people. They buy groceries, they buy supplies. You bring a scalloper with ten men on it and they go to the grocery store, their grub order might be $2,000. That's a nice sale. One-time sale to a grocery store. And they buy things from local businesses. You know, they buy refrigerators. These big boats have refrigerators, they have televisions, they have air conditioners. They're better equipped than my house. And they spend money. They have to. Especially for trip boats, it's their home away from home. These guys might be gone for two or three months from home, at a time.

Basically, I'm the only one that works during the week, and then I have somebody that comes in one day, Saturday, and another guy works Sunday, because we're open seven days a week. We have a bookkeeper, and we have an accountant. They have electricity, they have water. We sell fuel and ice. Various kinds of fishing supplies. I try to stock stuff that if they need to go fishing and the marine supply stores are closed, for instance, on a weekend or at night, and it's something they have to have to go fishing, I try and stock. We don't have the room to stock a lot, but we try to stock stuff like that. We don't have room for parts or anything like that. We have all the things needed to service the boat. Things like gloves and oilers and boots. You know. We're probably cheaper than most places. Because, as I say, we're not here to make a lot of money; we're here to help ourselves. We have to make something to pay the help and pay the overhead. Anything extra goes into maintaining the dock.

We have radio communication. We monitor the radio seven days a week, ten hours a day. So, we have constant contact at least with the boats that are within VHF range. And the fish buyers have a sideband that we have access to, if we have to talk to them on the sideband. And, of course, as I say, most of them have cellular phones, now.

The dock has opened at eight o'clock for years. Normally, if the boats are in, the boat owners will show up at eight, or before eight. And if it's a trip boat, and they're going to be in for a few days, they may have work to do, the crew may show up and mend nets or do maintenance on the boat. If they don't have anything to do, they just check the boat, make sure it's all right, and the captain may give them the rest of the day off. Or if all the work is done, he may tell them they don't even have to show up the next day if they're not planning to go fishing.

Dick Bardwell

"

Inside Stonington Fillet building.

"As far as taking out, we have a lot of radio communication. You've got side-bands, you've got VHF. Most of the boats have cellular phones, now, so you try to arrange to take out ahead of time. Of course, in the wintertime most boats come in because of the weather. More so than because they've got a trip. And you wait your turn. That's just the way it is. That's they way it is any place. So, other places it's much worse. You have to wait, sometimes, days. Maybe not so much now, but in years past when there were more boats.

A trip boat can stay out anywhere from two days to fourteen days, depending on what species they're fishing for or what kind of luck they're having. If they're fishing for flounder, they could take out as little as a couple hundred pounds, or even less. If they're fishing for squid, which is a low dollar value in comparison to flounder, they take out more than that. They take anything from a hundred pounds to five thousand, depending on what species and what's running, where they fished, their luck, the length of time they spend. And it changes daily.

Big variation with the trip boats. If they're fishing for what we call swill, soft fish–whiting, scup, or squid–you have to have a big trip to make any money at all. You're talking a fish that sells for fifty cents as opposed to a fish that sells for a dollar fifty, say. I've seen a lot of trips of a hundred thousand squid come in. I've seen a lot of trips of two or three thousand come in. Tremendous variation.

Most of the fish just comes off, it's weighed and sorted according to species and weight, and it's boxed. A lot of fish goes to Fulton Fish Market in New York, where there's umpteen buyers, and you send it to whatever buyer wants it, or whoever you've been dealing with. Some stuff like squid will go to freezer plants. It doesn't go directly to New York. Like flatfish used to go back to New Bedford because there were many, many cutting houses. I don't know what it's like there now, but there used to be 25 or 30 cutting houses in New Bedford, when there was a lot of yellowtail flounder and stuff around. But most of the flatfish is cut right here, now. Most of it goes to food and fish markets. Or with squid, sometimes it will go to big processor freezers. Sometimes scup will go to New Jersey or Philadelphia. And sometimes the flatfish will go back to New Bedford to be cut into fillets.

Of course, now you've got a Japanese market. Things like monkfish livers. Of course, a lot of tunafish goes to Japan. Fluke. Sometimes they'll bleed fluke at sea for sushi. They want real white meat. And that goes to Japan.

Dick Bardwell"

Joe Kessler stringing lobster bait.

"

Sometimes on the day they take out, if there's no congestion, they can take out, then they come back up and take their ice and fuel right then, if they're going to go out soon. In the wintertime, you don't have to worry about the ice melting, so you can take the ice right when you take the fish out. That way you go over, tie up, you're all set to go fishing the next time.

If you're going to be in for a few days, they'll usually take the fuel, because they need to know how much the fuel costs, so they can share up, when they get the check from the fish buyer. Then they'll come over just before they leave and take their ice. In the morning, if their boat's taking out, and they have trip boats, boats that have come in in the night, taken fish out in the morning, if there's no boats taking out you may have boats getting ready to go out coming over taking ice, or taking fuel and ice, loading groceries.

In the summertime, in the lobster season, you've got lobster boats constantly coming and going, because it's all fish the tide. They can only fish when there is a slack tide, when the buoys are up, if they're fishing where there's a strong tide. So, they come and go at all hours of the day to get fuel, take out lobsters. We get out-of-town boats from Montauk coming over to take fuel and ice.

Then, anytime from noon on, the day boats, depending on how long a day they put in, may start coming in and take out their fish. And they may or may not need supplies, depending on how many days they fished. Some of them can fish all week, and when what they consider their week is done, they take their fuel and ice so they know what their expenses were, so they can share up their fish checks. Some of them have to take fuel or ice, depending on what they're catching, every day or every couple of days.

And normally, they're in by six o'clock. Sometimes they'll pack later, if they have to. If there was particularly good fishing or something, they'll stay after six o'clock to pack the fish out. But as a rule, most everything's done. As I said, with the weather, when the weather's bad everybody seems to come at once, so sometimes we'll start early in the morning. They'll start taking boats out at four or five o'clock so they can get them all done in a day.

Dick Bardwell

"

Risks, Hardships, and Safety Measures

Widespread change has swept the commercial fishing industry over the past century, yet one factor, although unwelcome, has remained constant. Fishing remains one of the most hazardous occupations in the United States. A monument on the Stonington Town Dock, lists the names of 37 men from the fleet who have lost their lives at sea. It is a large toll for a small port, and it provides a solemn reminder of the risks facing Stonington's fishermen and lobstermen every day they are on board their boats.

Memorial wreath, Blessing of the Fleet.

Fishing remains a dangerous way to make a living, despite technological advancements, significant improvements in communication equipment, and better safety gear. Weather is a frequent adversary, particularly in the form of wind and vessel icing. In winter, if a fisherman goes overboard, frigid water temperatures can prove fatal in minutes. And the fishermen's close proximity to heavy equipment–and heavy cables, lines, and nets in an ever-moving environment–make accidents a constant threat. Increased catch restrictions and declining fish stocks may also impose indirect risks. A fisherman or lobsterman's economic situation may tempt him to go out alone or in poor weather, sacrificing personal safety for potential financial gain.

The boats do carry sophisticated and expensive safety gear, as mandated by U.S. Coast Guard regulations. Survival suits, life rafts, and good communication equipment do provide some measure of protection in the event of injury or accident. Still, the fishermen and lobstermen of Stonington are well aware that they work in a high-risk industry.

"

Every time they come out with a list of the most dangerous professions in the United States, commercial fishing's always at the top of the list. More people are injured and killed fishing than anything. You've got to love the water, you've got to love the independence. And you've got to be willing to make those kinds of sacrifices to be in the fishing business.

Dick Bardwell

We don't like to take unnecessary chances. I think men have gotten a lot better in the years. In the old days, they use to take those old crates out there. I don't know how they ever got back sometimes. Today I think they have gotten a lot more respect for the boats. Even though the boats are made of steel and things, they seem to pay more attention anyway. I know I do.

Thanks to our insurance companies and the Coast Guard, we have just about everything under the sun and it costs us dearly, believe me. It is good to have it. But I think a lot of it is nonsense. They go a little too far sometimes, although I guess they are doing it for our own good. But we have survival rafts, we have survival suits, we have flares. Our insurance companies come down and make sure that we have ample pumps on the boat, all kinds of safety equipment. Anything that you can imagine, we have to have. And we even have some of the things that we don't have to have.

Tim Medeiros

Everybody's required to have a survival suit, full suit. That's so if you get in the water–they're pretty insulated–you could live in them quite a while. We have an inflatable life raft, eight-man raft. So we have that, the survival suits, we have a thing we call an EPIRB, Emergency Position [-Indicating Radio Beacon] something, I'm not sure how it all goes. To a satellite or whatever. And that– it's pretty big–is very expensive too. We've got one of them that goes with you if you go on the raft. In the rafts they give you a little survival kit. So much drinking water, little things, pills, and stuff for food. It's pretty good. We do have our drills, you know. Everybody on the boat knows basically what they've got to do in an emergency. We have all kinds of alarms through the boat for fire, and high-water alarms in every compartment. And the boats today, they're pretty safe, you know. They're pretty safe boats, for the most part. The boat'll take care of itself. It's usually the guy who sinks it.

Jim Allyn

"

Seafarer approaching dock.

"

Well, I think right now she doesn't worry as much because of the safety equipment on the boats. She knows for a fact that we use our heads I'm sure that it's on her mind once in a while. You can have a nice calm day and something can happen or you can go overboard, that can happen. You can cross the street and get killed too. So I mean, she accepts that. But nowadays, if it's really blowing hard, nine out of ten times we're in. If we're caught in a breeze, yes, I think she worries but she also knows that as a rule, in this fleet nobody fishes alone.

Al Maderia

Today, yes, the crew is very well educated in what to do in an emergency. They've proven themselves several times, you know, on daily routine things that happen where most people would consider real bad, but it was no problem to them.

This boat we have now was brought in two winters ago with the net reel in the water, the whole main deck six feet under. They handled it very well. They still have the boat. They have immersion suits, they have life rafts, flares. We have a 405 kilohertz EPIRB which is, the signal is identified to your boat. There's all kinds of things. Plus, we have powerful radios. We can talk anywhere in the world with them. And there's a lot more vessels there.

But you do have sinkings. They happen. Things happen. Some things you can't prevent. And you have injuries. These hydraulic boats today, you get injuries. There's no way around it. It's like any other profession, or any other job, you're apt to get injured at any time. It can happen here just as well as there.

Walter Allyn

God forbid you have boats missing at sea. Boats are overdue and nobody's heard from them. Of course, everybody's on pins and needles until you hear from them one way or another. That's the worst thing. Well, you monitor the radio and everybody's really concerned. You tend to run from optimism to pessimism and back again. Depending on the conditions. The weather conditions, the condition of the boat. You know, everybody tries to second-guess what could have happened.

And then you have people lost overboard, which is another thing. So then you have a search. And most everybody will go out and search, say if it's local, if there's somebody lost overboard. Every once in a while you have a boat that will take on water at the dock or something. Hopefully that doesn't occur very often.

Dick Bardwell

"

Returning from wreath-laying, Blessing of the Fleet.

"

Two or three weeks ago, Arthur had a mine anchor. You know, had wires coming out of it. These are things that anchor the mines. I guess after a certain delay, they let the mine go or something. Second World War stuff. But you see wires coming out of an old rusty tube and you don't know whether it's a piece of a torpedo, or what it is. They sent the fire department and everything down here until the demolition guy got here from Newport and said, no, it's nothing to worry about. Then everybody went home. But that's not as common as it was. The stories before my time, you know, they're bringing in live torpedoes. Boats being blown up by torpedoes. I don't remember the names of them. I heard the stories, but that was during or shortly after the Second World War.

Dick Bardwell

Well, I was fishing in the wintertime, and I got caught in my net reel, the thing that winds up the net. And there was nobody there to stop it. I got cut. I was all chewed up and everything else. By some miracle, I wormed my way out of it after a couple of hours I guess it was, in the freezing cold. I managed to get to a radio, and they came and got me. But I swore I would never be out there alone again. I really thought it was the end. I never went out again after that alone. I was laid up for quite some time. I'm lucky that I've got all my moving parts and everything after what happened. And that is why I say it is a safety factor right now to have another man on my boat. It is set up to be run alone, and it is not hard work. But if one little thing goes wrong, and if there is not somebody there. You have to experience this to know what it is like. When you're in desperate need of help–I mean a live-or-die situation–and there is nobody there, just somebody to pull a lever that is out of your reach, it can mean everything to you. It is a hell of a feeling. I missed a couple of months. And then I forced myself to go to work. I didn't have any left arm for about a year. I had a man with me. That helped me out a lot. I couldn't have fished alone like that at all. You have to have both hands.

Tim Medeiros

"

John DeBragga.

"

I was pretty happy-go-lucky, didn't think too much about things. You go out and do your job and come in. This time, I was a goner. I don't know how I wasn't a goner. I thank God was there. He was there believe me, He heard me. There was nobody else there. After I got out of that thing, I called. They were aware that there was something wrong with me because I wasn't answering them. But of course, nobody knew exactly where I was. The other guys were offshore; most of the guys were offshore. There was one other fellow that was fishing inshore. He was already heading in. There was a couple of boats from the Point, but they were towing; they had no idea that there was anything wrong with me. My boat was headed out to sea, and the day was going on, it was getting dark. I managed to crawl in and got to the radio, and I just said, I told them at the dock, "I'm hurt, I'm on my way, have an ambulance standing by when I get there. I don't know how long it's going to take me." But somebody called the Coast Guard and they said, "You stop. Just stay right where you are. We'll come and we'll get you." And that is what they did. I don't know how long it took anybody to get there but they got there and that was the main thing. They took me in, towed my boat in after that. I was a mess. I saw my wife and my mother in the hospital. I tell you, I didn't think I was ever going to see them again. Nothing ever bothered me before, bad weather or anything like that. No problem. You've got faith in your boat, and your gear, and yourself, and things like that, but that was a little bit different.

Tim Medeiros

We've been accident-free. My oldest son did get hit in the head with a fragment of a block that carried away aloft. He was airlifted off the boat. This happened about six years ago, a hundred miles south of Montauk, in a nor'west gale in the winter. And his brother, the one that runs the *Matthew Melissa* now, put a call out at 11:57 in the morning to the Coast Guard. At 2:05 in the afternoon, he was at Waterford airport. His head was depressed an inch on one side. And due to the right action at the right time, and everything working fine, and the airlift and everything, I credit the youngster with saving his life. And the cooperation of the Coast Guard, and their ability with their helicopters and what-have-you. It was just amazing the way it happened. And the way he was cared for.

Walter Allyn

"

Richie Maderia and boat engine.

"Last winter we filled her up monkfishing. We had a malfunction in the alarm system down in my gear locker. The water comes up, the float lifts, the alarm goes off, lets you know there's water in there. But what happened was, I guess one of the connections got bad there and the thing didn't sound off. We were all torn up, ripped up one night. Got hung up and the net was ripped, and we spent four, five hours putting it together there in the middle of the night. And the boat was settling all the time. What had happened was a pump back-fed on us, with the engine running slow, she wasn't picking the suction up, what it was doing was back-flushing on us. Filled it right full. I had the whole stern underwater, I had to get the Coast Guard and all of that. We just kept steaming along there and the Coast Guard came up beside of us and they just ran along with us. And we eventually got it pumped out ourself. We were all right. A little nerve-racking that night.

It was bad night. We had 30-, 35-mile-an-hour winds; we were fishing in that 200-fathom edge and it's funny, you get out over that 100-fathom edge, it's a whole different world. The seas are just tremendous out there. They're spread out a little bit more, but they're huge, you know, and they're funny. They break different. They have a tendency to break like they would on a beach or a reef or something. Big rumblers, you know, and they can roll in down there. It's a pretty nasty area in the wintertime. You fish out there, you better have a good boat out there, that deep water. You've gotta pay your dues out there.

Jim Allyn

Yeah. We were in a close call a few years back. We were about a 110 miles south of here. And we had a locker fill up. It was a gale going, and all the boats were laying to, and we had a locker fill up with water underneath the deck. We didn't know it. The alarm wasn't working properly, the battery was dead or some malfunction happened, and we didn't know that the locker was full of water. And we were laying for some reason. Because of the weather, I believe. And we ended up putting it back into gear, and she just laid right over. And we were aware of the situation at that point. So, we had a close call there. The stern was real low. Took us a long time to pump it out. But I think, I believe that night the *Lois Joyce* sank. Same night. We were on our way in, we were ahead of him. And they all survived on that boat, but I think a similar thing happened to them. A locker filled up and just tipped her right over.

Phil Torres"

John Rita.

"We were in back of Fishers Island and a violent thunderstorm came down the back side of the island. We were in the process of hauling our net back, to go home. But it came on us so quick. And a bolt of lightning hit the top antenna. It made an explosion. When it hit, it just blew, and the next thing, we were on fire.

John Rita

The time it burned was '78 because I was nine months pregnant with my daughter. I rode down and I saw a boat coming in smoking, and I didn't recognize it at the time. And he was all smoky and everything and I didn't stay down there. But they were safe. That's all that mattered.

Ann Rita

We got a phone call from my grandfather, and he had heard from somebody who was monitoring the VHF. The *Rosemary R.* was coming, in flames, and we went right down, and we saw the towboat towing it in. And we got word that my father was safely on the towboat. And for the next two or three hours just watching firemen go in and out, and put out the flames. It was a mixture of being very thankful that nobody was hurt, and realizing, or not even really realizing, what a setback it would be, financially, for the family.

Michael Medeiros

It was a windy day, out of the southeast. He was right ahead of us. And he was doing some rolling. He was really laying her over. And we just happened to be right close to them on the way in. She rolled again, and she just kept going. And it was December. It was cold. It was just a miracle that we were able to save those two men. I never thought we would.

John Rita

You have to understand what can happen, but almost have blinders on to it. It seemed to me if you thought too much about falling overboard, if you thought too much about the weather, you'd lose the edge in fishing and you wouldn't be aggressive enough. So, it's respect mixed with a little innocence.

Michael Medeiros"

Fishermen at Home and Family Life

Mike Grimshaw and his daughter.

For many fishermen, the work they do is more than a job; it is a way of life. It affects their lives, and the lives of their families, far beyond the time they spend on their boat or at the dock. It influences many family activities, including such basic routines as sleep and meal patterns. Fishermen are likely to be away from home for many hours each day, or if they are on trip boats they will be gone for days at a time. Their work schedule often limits their involvement in family activities. They often miss their childrens' activities and other events. Their long absences place an added burden on their wives, who must manage their households alone for extended periods.

The financial aspects of fishing create added stress for families. Income is unpredictable and often decreases sharply during the winter. Families must budget for periods of limited income caused by such factors as seasonal movements of fish and poor weather. Fishermen and lobstermen function as independent businessmen, and as a result they don't receive benefits from an employer. They are not eligible for unemployment compensation and they must provide their own health insurance. The financial health of the family depend upon the fisherman's success, and increased regulation means less earning potential.

Family members often take an active role in support of fishermen or lobstermen. They may help paint and maintain boats, string lobster bait, manage financial records, or actually go out on the boats and participate. Children often participate, working with their fathers during their summer vacation from school. Families also provide moral support, accepting what is in many ways a difficult lifestyle.

"You did whatever needed to be done, out of necessity. I was alone all the time. And in those days he was gone, whether he'd be out to sea all the time or in another port, he'd be gone ten days to two weeks. And so, I had to be both mother and father. And you just took it in your stride. And I think being as young as I was, it was easier. I wouldn't want to do that today. And you just did what you had to do. You didn't know any different, so you didn't complain about it and you just did it.

And I think the most difficult times were when the children were sick or got hurt. I remember one instance where my oldest had just gone to kindergarten, and she brought home measles and chicken pox to the others. And that was six weeks that I didn't stick my nose out the door, except to hang clothes. The groceries were delivered to the house. And at one point I remember calling my mother and asking her to come, in tears, just to sit for a few minutes while I took a walk. Because I felt like the whole house was closing in on me. It was just almost more than you could take. Then they all ended up with tonsillitis. So, it was a bad time.

Well, you worried a lot. And you just hoped everything was okay. And it was just a way of life. And you never liked it, but you became accustomed to it. You had to, you had to go on with your everyday life for the children. I'm sure it would have been different if I hadn't had children. But with the children, they were my whole world, really. Because I was alone so much. Just take care of them. It was very hard. And as far as the children were concerned, you know, they were almost like strangers to him when they were little, because he wasn't around very much.

Betty Fellows

He was doing both. He was working at EB [Electric Boat], he worked the night sift. He'd get up at eleven o'clock and go in at midnight. And then when he'd come home in the morning, he'd get ready to go out lobstering. So by the time he got home in the afternoon, he could get those few hours of sleep. We had to be quiet. You know, "Dad needs his sleep," and we knew it. So being seven of us, we knew how to keep it quiet. We didn't see my dad that much because he did work hard. I understand it more now than I did when I was younger. And I understand what he was working for.

My mother always had our family meals together. I mean before he went to bed, we used to basically have dinner around five o'clock. And that's when right after dinner, he'd go up to bed for a few hours. We always had our dinner together. That was like, we're going to do something together and that will be the meal, and that's what we did."

Ann Rita

John and Ann Rita and children.

"

It has to be a special family. I mean, not too many people get up and go to work and they're gone for four days, or five days. And they come home the next week, and here I am again. Couple of days later they're gone for four days. A lot of people are used to nine-to-five. It takes a lot of getting used to. The kids take a lot. I've got two kids and they don't want to see me leave, but they're happy to see me come back. One's six and one's ten. One girl, one boy. The boy's the youngest. I try to stay in touch. I've got the cellular phone and I've got the sideband, so I can be reached if anything happened or I had to be reached. Yeah, she's on her own for four days, five days, or whatever. And, like I say, it takes a lot. Not everybody could do it.

Manny Soares

When I got married, the only thing I didn't want was tripping. And I said, "You can fish all you want. I don't mind the one, two days but don't go on a trip boat." You know, I see it and I don't like it. And he didn't like it so it worked out really good. I think, like I said, you have to know what you're getting into. You're going to be mother and father for three-quarters of the time. No, not for me. Some people can do it and I see it. They seem to be pretty good. Some of them don't make it. And I think that the reason is that they probably just didn't see what they were getting into. I mean, tripping is hard, you've really got to manage things really well, even moneywise.

Being the bookkeeper down there, I get to know a lot of people. There are a few families down there that I see, you see them on the dock waving goodbye, knowing they're not coming back for seven to ten days. I couldn't live that life, and I wonder how can they? They have families, small kids, and then they're only home for four or five days. And you don't know if they're going to be home for Christmas, Thanksgiving. You know they're not going to be home for the kids' birthdays, or special things that the kids have to attend to, school happenings. But I would think that they would have to know before they get into the marriage that this is the way it's got to be. And I'm sure most of them do.

Ann Rita

Well, I guess adaptability is a big thing. Like my son who runs the *Matthew Melissa*, he's gone for 10, 12 days at a clip. His wife maintains the house, manages the children, does what she has to do. And when he comes home, he's home for three or four, five days, whatever. Time off, per year, I would say he has as much or more than the guy working on the beach. It works out. My wife survived. My sons' wives survive. The children are there, they go to school, like everybody else.

Walter Allyn

"

Jim Allyn and family in exhibit tent.

"

It's tough on the family life, you know. I've got three kids and a wife. I'm not home all the time. It's tough on her. It's a tough business. It's just something you've got to get used to. The tough part for her is, you know, she's got to do all the disciplinarian stuff with the kids. It gets tough; the kids miss you. And you come home and the first two days home, you're kind of like jet-lagged out. And you finally get into the way of life on land again and it's time to go. You know, you get burned right out.

Jim Allyn

We always have supper together unless I'm going to be a little bit late. Sometimes I'm falling asleep at the table, but we manage to eat.

Well, we hear that a lot here. "Why don't you get a job like a normal person?" With the children it is tough, they have things at school that they have to go to. If my wife wasn't here to do it, they have to miss out on it. Because I don't work nine-to-five. I don't work eight hours a day. It takes up 14 or 15 hours of the day, every day. We like to think that we are compensated well for it, but that hasn't been the case. Sometimes yes, sometimes no. It may even out in the long run.

Last winter was the worst. The worst year I've ever had fishing. We still manage to keep our heads above water and make a living. As a matter of fact, last year, we sat here and ate up every ounce of every penny we had saved up over the years just to make it through the winter. That's how bad it was.

Tim Medeiros

He spent the whole first part of his career as a fisherman going out for five or six days in a row. I've heard that his reputation was, when he took a boat out, it didn't come back until it had a trip. And if there was no fish, and no price, he would stay out for two weeks or more, and fish through whatever weather, and go into ports at night, and fish in the lee side of an island, where no one else would go. And then I think that he felt he missed a lot of my sisters' growing up. And when I was born he started day tripping. You're home every night, except for a couple of exceptions in the winter. And you get more ties with the land, and more ties with your family. I think that's a certain mellowing for a day tripper. Especially for someone who's so used to just going away and not seeing his wife or kids for a week at a time.

Michael Medeiros

"

Taking out at Stonington Fillet.

"

I got used to seeing somebody come home in various moods. And I can remember when he used to sell in Greenport, Long Island, he'd come back–they'd go once a week at that time–he'd come back on Fridays around three o'clock in the afternoon. And he'd still be disgusted after the two-hour trip back because he had to yell and scream at the fish buyer for a nickel higher in price per pound. And it seemed like, because the pay fluctuates, you never know what to expect. And payday was always interesting, wondering how dad would come home. But it was a heck of a way to grow up.

You never plan on eating together, that's for sure. Especially, the winter months. They go offshore and either they would go into Montauk for the night, or my father would come home seven, eight o'clock, and he'd eat dinner then, and I'd eat whenever. You're really used to your father, even being a little kid, your father goes to bed before you do. Eight o'clock he's in bed and he's ready. And if he sees nine o'clock some nights, that's a big deal. A lot of compromises that I never really realized he was making. And I never really realized he was working so hard. When I played little-league baseball, seemed like whenever there was a big game, he was there. And then as I learned more about his schedule, I realized he came in early for those days–and he lost money to make sure that he could come in and see those things–which I didn't really realize at the time. It's something special looking back on it now.

And I still don't really like lobster that much, because all summer long there are lobsters in the fridge for you to eat whenever you want one, and as a result I got really spoiled by it, and I really don't like them. I do like fish. I love eating fish. And my father could eat it seven days a week. He loves flounder, codfish, anything like that.

The biggest positive for me, personally, was realizing that when times were tough or times were great, my father loved his job. And that's something I picked up early on, and I carry with me. And I will for the rest of my life. You have to love what you do. And you can't fish unless you love it. It would just be hell to be out there and not want to be there. And I saw my father, saw how much he loved working. He'd rather be on the boat than on shore any day; never liked to take any vacations. And it meant a lot to me that he could have taken a different route and had more free time, but he didn't want to. It was very uplifting to see somebody who really, truly enjoyed what they do.

Michael Medeiros

"

Disadvantages and Negative Aspects

John Rita.

Fishermen generally seem to accept the long hours, hard work, risks, and often harsh environment that has always characterized their industry. The are less accepting of time away from family. Most seem to agree that the greatest disadvantage they face is increased regulation and the limiting effect it has on their independence and earning potential, traditionally two of the most appealing aspects of their chosen way of life.

"

I know we have a tough job. In my household, I grew up with it, and my wife grew up with it, and it's a way of life. But I don't think people know what I go through. There are times it's just a tough, tough thing living it sometimes. Not even financially, but just what you have to do. Who wants to get out of bed when the temperature is zero, at three o'clock in the morning? Not many. It's long hours. I don't think people actually realize.

John Rita

The worst things are when something happens aboard the boat and you lose a guy. That to me is about the worst. It can't be any worse than that. Because I blame myself all the time. It's always there, never gets away. Stays there. And I bleed when something like that, like Georgie Roderick. He was taking in the bag of fish, and the block busted from the hoister and hit him right in the head and killed him right off. Things like that. I was doing the talking with the Coast Guard for him and everything on my boat. Those are the worst things.

Get caught in a storm, and you're plugging away, and you got to slow down because you got to go. Conditions of the weather, just like out on the road, when you're driving. Use a little common sense. Sometimes you can make it in two, three hours. Sometimes it takes you ten, twelve hours to get the same distance. But you're safe. You're going slow. But you're always thinking and worried. So, that's about the worst when you get caught in a storm, a real bad one. I got caught in a few of them.

Jim Henry

As far as what is bad about being a lobsterman, you can't stay up late at night, especially during the summertime. There are a lot of activities with the kids and for myself, we'd like to go out and enjoy ourselves at night. You know, go out to dinner. Gets to be about nine o'clock, it's time to go to bed. "Let's go to a movie, let's go to the drive-in." Aren't many drive-ins left, I know. I used to enjoy things like that. Can't do it.

I used to like to go to the races, stock-car races. If I have the next day where I know I'm fishing the tide area that I have to leave maybe at nine o'clock in the morning or something, then I can go do that. Mind you I've been up since quarter after three. And I'd be there with my head kind of nodding on my chest, and the guy next to me said to my wife one time, "How the heck can he sleep through that?" "Well, he's been up since three o'clock this morning." You know, stuff like that. You want to stay up late and have a good time with the kids. Or during the summertime you'd like take your kids to the beach. I mean, I haven't been to the beach all summer. I was on the water every day, but it just wasn't at the beach with my kids. You know, they're out having a good time and stuff, and I'm not there to enjoy it. That part I miss.

"

Mike Grimshaw

Walter Allyn (L) and Jim Allyn.

"

They tell me I'm pretty cranky this time of year. There's a wind-down period from the adrenaline, the hype, from fishing all summer. And then we take off, me and my wife, with no kids for a short time. Three, four days, usually around the 10th of October, and kind of wind down. Now I have a little bit of a life. I go to football practice with the kids, and go to their games and stuff. I can have a more normal kind of life. More of a nine-to-five kind of deal. In the winter, it slows down. I like it. It just slows down. I can enjoy the kids. I mean, I look at a picture like the one behind you there, my daughter. She's little there. I look at her now, it's like she's three going on thirty.

Mike Grimshaw

Health insurance is a big issue. We have to have our own health insurance. That is very, very costly. We've juggled health insurance companies; we've probably had five or six of them over the years. They get so high, you've got to give up this and that. We finally resolved that we have it but it is not what we'd like to have, but it is what we can afford today. The good plans are way out of whack. Other things are, if something happens to one of us, we get sick or something, we don't get paid to stay home. No one takes our boat fishing; no one sends you a check for staying home if you're sick, or if you get injured. That is probably the worst fear. It is probably my worst fear, is if something happened. If I had a heart attack or if I got injured or something, what would happen around here? The older you get the more you think about that. The bills go on and they don't really care one way or another what is happening. Some people will let somebody take their boat and run it. But I have found that is usually not a very smart thing to do. Maybe sometimes it is, but usually it's not.

The other things, the hours, there's a lot of hours. How does it affect the family? Well it does. You are not with your family a lot. There's a lot of things you can't do, that you like to do with the children. Holidays don't correspond with theirs. When they get a day off, we don't take days off. We fish holidays, weekends, and weather. What else can I say? Insurance bills.

Tim Medeiros

"

Coming in.

"

Right now, if you're a fisherman, you're considered self-employed so you don't have unemployment, you don't have health insurance. Right now, that's a big thing. When I first started fishing in the fifties, Blue Cross cost me $18.00 for three months, and I think the CMS [major medical insurance], or whatever, was $9.00. So, it was no problem. Unemployment, you know, you had to pay it then, but you never used it. You only got $45.00 every two weeks. Because back then you were only making a hundred bucks, hundred and fifty bucks was good money. But that's all changed now. Now, your medical insurance.... Last I had, I had to cancel and switch to another company. I was paying like $3,000 for three months.

Robert Berg

Prices. To me, it's the only tough part. The toughest thing for us to understand today is the prices. Inflation calls for everybody's job to get more money. In the lobster business it's gone the other way. We get less and less for the lobsters. That's the toughest part.

Richie Maderia

Part I don't like, well, I don't know, I like most it. But no matter what job you have, if the money isn't there then you kind of get discouraged; I guess that's it. Everything else I like. I don't mind the hard work, you know, like tearing nets, things like that, that goes with part of the job. But if you're doing something you like and when you've done real well through the years and all of the sudden you're not, well that would have to be the part. I'd like to see us doing better than we are right now. But outside of that, the hours, the work, none of that bothers me.

Arthur Medeiros

"

Advantages and Benefits of Fishing

Seafarer at the Blessing of the Fleet.

Fishing is a difficult means of making a living, yet many fishermen can't imagine doing anything else. A number of them have pursued other types of work, especially indoor work, and it has made them miserable. They love being outdoors. They cherish the flexibility and sense of freedom. And family support and tradition often give them an increased sense that they are doing what they should be doing.

"

I took on another job at the American Velvet Company in between this. I worked in the Velvet Company in the dye house for ten years. I became the general foreman of the place. But I progressed as high as I could make it in the place and I couldn't stand it. I just had to get out. I am wondering if I made the right choice today, but I love what I do and I guess that means a lot.

Tim Medeiros

I tried EB [Electric Boat] a couple of times. I just couldn't take it. I just didn't like it. It just wasn't for me. I just didn't fit in there. I wanted to fish more than I wanted to work ashore. There was a certain freedom that I enjoyed, so I tell myself anyway. And there was some kind of satisfaction in knowing, whether I was successful or a failure, everything I did was directly related to me. I couldn't blame anybody else for it. So, consequently, I've always been a commercial fisherman, other than a few years I did lobstering while my daughter was growing up and I came ashore.

Joe Rendeiro

It's a clean living. It's a clean, honest living. It is really. I couldn't think of a cleaner, or more honest way to make a living. It's hard work, but you're rewarded for it.

Jim Allyn

Sometimes you take a deep breath, and you go, "Boy what else would you rather be doing than being out here like this?" You do have days like that. Not a lot. There's a few. I take a lot of guys out with me. They like to just go out and see what it is like. They say, "Oh, this is great. Oh, man, I love this. I'd give up that job any day to do this." Everybody seems to love it. It makes you feel good, too, when people say that. It is almost like they are envious of you in a way.

Tim Medeiros

It is pretty much a thrill. I love it. Every time I go out it's a thrill for me. And I've been doing it for a few years now. I think about, wow, in ten years you'll look back on this and say, "Wow, what a thrill."

Phil Torres

I'm the boss. No one is telling me what to do. Between the ocean, which I love, and me being the boss of my own business, this is the way I want to do things. There's nothing better than that. You know, if I don't feel well at five o'clock in the morning, I'll go back to sleep for another hour, I'll go out at six o'clock. Great feeling. No time clock. I might put in an extra hour that day because of it, but at least that was my decision. It was totally my decision. That's what I like. I love lobstering for that. I make my own time. I do what I've got to do. So, I'm happy about it.

"

Richie Maderia

Rosemary R.

"

I enjoy being out all the time. I enjoy it. Oh yeah, we just enjoy the scenery just like everybody else. Like somebody being on a sailboat or a yacht, we feel the same way. You just like the feeling of being on the water. I like the independence, I like the phrase of being free as a bird; I can't put it any simpler than that. It's a good feeling, doing what you like, being out in the fresh air, being your own boss. Even when people work for you, it's still like being your own boss. There's no punching the time clock or people standing over you. It's just different. It's something you have to do I guess, and like.

Arthur Medeiros

When I was fishing with him, every morning we'd be working putting out the net, and it seemed like for a few weeks there we had just finished setting the net right when the sun was coming up. And I'd spend a few extra minutes on deck, just watching it. And you'd only see a couple other fishing boats around, the sea would be calm, and it was amazing. There were a few special mornings when my mood was just right, and the sunrise was just right, and everything came together, and it didn't really matter what was happening on shore. The whole time I was out there, you're entirely separated from everything going on, all the people back home, and a lot of times that's a great feeling. It's really nice to know you're away from everything and it's not going to hit you again, till you come back home.

Michael Medeiros

The best thing, in my opinion, is just the freedom. It's being out there. It's knowing that you are responsible. You and your captain, or your crew, are responsible for every penny in your paycheck. And when you do well, there's so much pride in knowing that you worked for all of that money. And that's something a lot of people don't understand. It's not a job where you can just go through the motions and do well, or if you have an off week, you're still going to receive your same hourly pay, or whatever. No. You're not going to get anything. And the bills are still going to come. So, it's real rewarding when you have a good day, and you come home, and you're exhausted, but you know that you did everything you could today. And you had a heck of a day. Unfortunately, the way the industry is, there aren't that many good days anymore. But when you get one it's really special.

Michael Medeiros

You're outside. You gotta like it, being outside. I love the outside.

Al Maderia

"

Taking out at Stonington Fillet.

"

I think there is prestige in it, in some respect. I feel good about what I do. A lot of times, people say, "Oh, you are a fisherman?" I feel good about it. I like the freedom of it. I used to be able to say that you could probably make as much money as you wanted to make. It is not really the case anymore. You can still call your shots, though, in certain respects. What else? The fresh air. It's nice, you know? When I was cooped up in the factories, I didn't like that. No, not at all. You feel good. You come home at night, especially if you've had a good day's catch. I do anyway. I feel great. I did something, I did it myself. It wasn't anybody else's machinery or something that did it for me. When I get the check at the end of the week, and especially if it is a good one, it makes you feel good.

Tim Medeiros

Well, the best thing in fishing is the money. When you make a good week's pay, that's the best thing of fishing.

Jim Henry

The best thing's probably independence.

Robert Berg

I just like working out in the open air. You're your own person. When times are good, there's no limit on what you can make. I guess what you put into it is what you get out of it. If you build something right, it's going to last. If you don't, you're going to do it twice. I just like being free, your own person.

John Rita

Your own boss. You get to go and come as you please. If you want to go, you go. If you don't, you can take time off if you want.

Other than the regulations, I think it's pretty much how it used to be. Once you get out there. As I said, I like to fish.

Manny Soares

It's just one thing after the other. Whereas, if you are employed by somebody, you don't have these worries. But then you get a beautiful day sometimes, and you are out in your boat, and you are catching fish, and you forget about all that stuff. You say, "To hell with it, I don't need it." I love it. This is it, you know?

Tim Medeiros

I think commercial fishermen fish because they want to fish. They're there because they want to be there. It's a way of life. They enjoy this way of life. They get personal satisfaction out of this way of life.

Walter Allyn

Just being out there. It's beautiful out there on the water. And it's so peaceful and calm. There's no one there to bother you. You make your own time. You know, you do what you have to do. He has one guy working with him, and they get their job done. You don't have somebody leaning over your shoulder and telling you what to do, and this has got to be done, that's got to be done. And it's beautiful out there.

Ann Rita

"

Fishermen cleaning up the dock.

Bishop Reilly blesses the *Lady Lynn*.

Traditions

The Stonington fishing fleet is rich in tradition. These traditions center around family, community, religion, and the Portuguese heritage of many of the fleet members. Traditions are extremely important to many of the men and their families. These traditions provide a foundation for the often-challenging fishing lifestyle, and they help transform fishing from a job or business, to a way of life.

Fishing ranks as one of the most ancient activities in the history of the human experience and one of the oldest forms of commercial enterprise in America. It is an industry rich in tradition, which is not surprising considering its long history and its significance. For the Stonington fishermen, some traditions evolved locally and some, such as religious traditions, have their roots in the Old World. Regardless of their source, traditions are an important component of the fishing way of life.

In a sense, the most basic tradition is the fisherman's relationship with his environment. The seascape has remained largely unchanged through time and is an element of fishing that links the past and present. A fisherman going to sea today is surrounded by essentially the same natural environment that was observed by fishermen 100 and more years ago. It is a traditional view. The sky, the clouds, and the sun appear the same. So do the ocean water and swells. The birds are the same, as are the profiles of the islands and southern New England coast. Although the details ashore are drastically different and the boats on the water have evolved, a fisherman from 100 years ago would recognize the environment.

"

Fishermen are so superstitious. You were not allowed to say the word "pig" on the boat. I'm not really sure where that superstition comes from, but my father and John both stick to that. If somebody says "pig" on the boat, they know something horrible is going to happen within the next day. And every time I'd lift up a hatch cover, my father would remind me not to flip it upside down, because that's also very bad luck. And I suppose, whether it's articulated or not, thinking about what can go wrong is a superstition. Maybe it will go wrong if you think about it too much.

Michael Medeiros

Some old things never go away. Like I never turn my hatches upside down. That's supposed to mean bad luck, your boat will sink. And stuff like that, yeah, you just don't talk about it, but still there's some of the old traditions still there.

Mike Grimshaw

I was very aware of it, personally. I knew that I was just another person in my family going through, learning the exact same things. And I think most fishermen are aware of it, although some of them don't recognize that fact. Fishermen love to tell stories about the old days, and I love to hear every one of them. It's the same water, it's the same coast, and I could hear stories of my father from 40 years ago, when he was about my age, and really understand and know what was happening even though I wasn't there. And in that sense, the oral tradition gets passed along. Everyone knows it, and everyone adds to it. So, they know what's going on even if they don't recognize it as a certain tradition.

Michael Medeiros

"

Community Traditions

Mike Pacheco.

Some Stonington residents dislike the presence of the fishing fleet. Perhaps unaware of the town's important fishing heritage, they would prefer a more fully residential Stonington Borough, with no industrial complex on the waterfront and no truck traffic throught the streets. Yet fishing holds an important place in Stonington's history, and fishing remains a distinctive part of the community today. The fleet contributes significantly to the color and character of the town. The community fishing traditions are of course most evident at the dock itself, and the boats and facilities of the fleet are an integral part of the harbor.

The fleet and the Town Dock provide various benefits to town residents. The fishermen and lobstermen provide much in demand fresh seafood to area markets and restaurant. One local fishing family now operates a restaurant of their own, featuring traditional Portuguese seafood dishes. The fishermen's memorial and an observation area at the dock provide the public with a pleasant site for enjoyment of the waterfront. And many area residents enjoy the pageantry, speciality foods, and music during the annual Blessing of the Fleet, even if they do not enjoy the influx of people and cars into Stonington Borough.

The fishermen themselves take an active role in the greater community, even if they can no longer afford to live in the Borough near the waterfront. Several are members of the volunteer fire department. Others serve on town committees, especially those relating to the waterfront. The Holy Ghost Society building, an active gathering place and social club, stands as a reminder of the longstanding, significant Portuguese presence in the town. In all, the Stonington fishing fleet and its members are obviously part of, not separate from, the town.

"

You had the mills, you had the Atwood Company, a machine company, and you had various small businesses, but basically, Stonington was known as a fishing community. We had a lot of Portuguese people, and most of them were fishermen. I can't think of a family that wasn't somehow related to fishing. Somebody was connected to fishing, almost, in every family. And, of course, we had the velvet mill, and we had the weavers,.... but to me, if I think of Stonington in my youth, I think of fishing. A lot of fishermen lived on the water, down on the Point. Fishermen owned the homes that everybody wants now. They were owned by fishermen. All the homes along Water Street, down around the Point. They wanted these homes in these areas, so that they could see the weather every day. They kept track. They'd get up in the morning, stick their head out the back door; if the weather suited them they'd go fishing. If it didn't, they wouldn't go. And the manner in which they went fishing. Then, a skipper would get up, look at the weather, then you go around knock on the doors of his crew. And they'd meet down the boat.

I wouldn't know what the percentage would be, but whenever we had the Holy Ghost Celebration, the town would be packed. I would say, from the Cannon Square south, I would venture to say 95 percent of the people were Portuguese. But we had a lot of Portuguese people in town, the Borough was basically Portuguese.

It was playing in the shipyard, playing on the boats. Like a lot of boats where the condominiums were built in Stonington; a lot of the fishermen would haul their boats up there for repair. So, our big deal would to go up there and play fisherman. You know, on the boats. On the old lobster boats that were still tied up, and were in the slips. If the fishermen weren't there, we'd go down to the lobster boats and fool around. Or, maybe, if we were lucky, one of those guys would pay us fifty cents or a quarter to help him string his bait or something like this. We had jobs like that when we were kids. You know, if you make fifty cents, wow! That took you two weeks to the movies in Westerly, because it cost a quarter to go to the movie. Or when the Community Center opened up, it cost like fifteen cents to go to a movie in the Community Center. So, if you got a little job doing that. A lot of times we were run off the boats because we either broke something or misplaced something, were playing with it, that the boat owner couldn't find. But, basically, that's what we did.

Joe Rendeiro

"

Joe Rendeiro.

"

We went down around the docks and come suppertime, six o'clock, you got yourself home to eat. Or especially, if you saw your father coming. Everybody could recognize the boats. I could recognize my father's boat from way off: the mast configuration and things like that. And soon as he come in, we'd go run down there and be with him. Help him unload his fish or whatever. Hang around the boat. That's basically what it was. On Fridays, whenever he was there, Friday was the day they did their maintenance network, and they did the sharing up. That's what I'd do, I'd hang around the boat with the old man.

There were a lot of families. Families would come here and spread the news that there was a good living to be made here, and the rest of the family would come over here. A lot of them. Like you take the Maderia family. That's a great big family. The Roderick family. They were some of the biggest families in town, as far as Portuguese people go. And there were others. Even though the names are not the same, you know, sisters married other people. They get different names, but they're still related, but without the same name. Yes, there was a lot of that. It was a very close community, the Portuguese community. If you went down the Portuguese Club 30 years ago, you would find Portuguese people. I'm talking about the old mustachioed boys with the handlebar mustache, playing pinochle or something like that, and drinking nickel beers. If you go to a Portuguese club today, you don't see that. It's not the society that it was back in the old days.

Things have changed. I think they're trying to maintain the heritage that goes with this Portuguese club, but somehow or other it's not the same. I think myself, today, the Portuguese club is maintained specifically as an economical place to drink. Or something like that. It doesn't mean the same thing to the younger people that it did to the old-timers. The Portuguese club back then was known as the Holy Ghost Society. You know, it had a lot to do with the beliefs of the Catholic religion, the famine in Portugal, and all that stuff that took place. And these people brought that heritage with them from the old country, you know, from the islands. We had people from the Azores, the Madeiras, and then the mainland. It was a mixture of Portuguese people from different parts of Portugal and different islands, Portuguese possessions. So, they had a pretty good cross section of Portuguese people living there.

Joe Rendeiro

"

George McCagg.

"

I never thought about things like discrimination or things like that. I don't think anybody ever pointed out that, because I was Portuguese, I was something less than they were. I never walked around with a chip on my shoulder looking to prove I was better than anybody else or somebody's equal. I never had that problem. It was just a good time. The hardest time I had in Stonington was school. I didn't like school. I wanted to do everything that you couldn't do in school. That's all. I couldn't get out of school fast enough. I'm not saying I was a bad student, I just didn't pay attention in school. That's why I didn't get very far in school. I didn't want to do anything that school would get me. I wanted to go fishing. I wanted to go in the navy when the war was going on, and after the war, I just wanted to go back fishing again. And I knew that my father or anybody I chose to ask would teach me all the things the school couldn't teach me, and that's what I wanted to do.

Joe Rendeiro

They can't afford the houses, the old people. The Portuguese had to get out, The taxes drove them out.

Robert Berg

I can remember years ago, catching herring down at Bindloss's. Where this outfit from Maine would open trailers, big long trailers, and we'd unload the herring off the boats and dump them in these big barrels and they'd run the barrels up with hand trucks up a plank to the trailer. They'd fill it up, I mean fill it, until it was overflowing. And the trailer truck would go out of Stonington, and it would be spilling herring right up all the streets. Nobody ever made a complaint. Everybody was happy with it, you know. Try that today and, man. So you got an awful lot of people in Stonington that came because it's a quaint old fishing town. But, it's like everything else, they want to change it, you know?

Charlie Fellows

I had quite a few friends in Stonington and always liked the people in Stonington, the Yankee stock and the Portuguese stock. I have a great deal to say on the plus side about Portuguese. They were very fine people. And they're quiet and very modest and nice people to get along. The Yankees are, too, you know, but I know those Portuguese. And the Portuguese schooner I worked on was really nice. But there was the fishing fleet that had their circle. And then, they had the Atwood Machine. A lot of people worked there. And then the velvet mill, they worked up there. And so, you had the people that were manufacturing and the people that were fishing. And though they knew each other and were very sociable, they seemed to keep to their own fraternities. The fishermen were always talking fish, you know. And I don't know what the other people in Atwood's, but I suppose they were talking about molding sand and stuff like that.

Arthur Griffin

"

Charlie and Betty Fellows.

"

I used to live on Hancock Street. I could come up Hancock Street, go up Diving Street, go the back street. And most any house, people outside, "Hey, you want any coffee?" Everybody was so friendly. The rich people of those days, they were very, very friendly. There was no complaints whatsoever. In fact, when we first started fishing the bigger boats, Stonington Boat Yard built the boats. Hank Palmer used to build them there. They used to put on the mufflers, they were very loud. The rich people, we used wake them up. They offered to buy us mufflers to put on there, so it wouldn't wake them up at nighttime. That's how good those people were. They were very good. They wouldn't just complain, like some people. No, they were right there to help you out if they could.

Jim Henry

That's all it was. Mainly a fishing town. There just aren't any around anymore. I don't know of anybody in town here that used to be a fisherman, my age or anything. There's no fishermen around here. I'm the only one.

Manny Maderia

My wife's family, her father, "Sleepy" Maderia, he fished. His father fished. Up the road, the Arrudas fished. Down on the corner, of course, Arthur's uncle, Danny Cidale. The Rodericks. Everybody fished. Rendeiros. The whole gang. That was it.

You could go down to the dock, on any given day, if somebody had net-work to do back then, there was all kinds of people to help. Now, I guess, life is so much quicker, and everybody just goes down and does their work, jumps in the vehicles and they're off. And, I guess, that's your problem. Not all but most have their own thing going in life today. But back then there wasn't that many cars. Everybody walked down for everything going in Stonington. Everything in Stonington you wanted, grocery stores, package stores, barbershops. Everybody just walked around. But most of the fishermen, yes, they helped. They were tight knit, definitely.

John Rita

Not enough children like years ago. Now, at the end of the village here, we had Portuguese families. And they came over right from Portugal. And they would get over and get a job, and bring somebody else over, their brothers, or sisters, or somebody like that. And down just below the cannons, there were hundreds of them there. And they were big families. And almost all of them was fishing. They had their small boats. Then there were lobster boats, and they had their lobster pots which they made themselves. And we had fishermen going around selling, and then we had a fish market.

Frank Keane

"

John Rita (L) and Jim Henry organizing parade.

"

There were a lot of small boats, then, and maybe two people working on them. And maybe father and the son, or maybe brothers, or something like that. But it was a big fishing fleet. And it was a flourishing town. I mean, they bought all the grub here in town. And when they went out, they ate. We had maybe six or eight grocery stores and a couple fish markets. And we had one, two, three, four barbershops. You know, the fishing people don't mean anything anymore. I mean, around here. They just own a boat, and they go fishing for a livelihood. They don't have the presence. There's a fishing fleet here in town, but it isn't like it used to be. What I mean is, well, they really supported the town, but not today.

Frank Keane

It was a close-knit community where most of them were fishing people. Everybody out of Stonington fished. That's what most of the people did. It was a very nice community. Especially to grow up in.

John Rita

"

Miss Karyn approaching the dock.

The Blessing of the Fleet

Bishop Reilly blessing boats.

The annual Blessing of the Fleet marks the high point of tradition associated with the Stonington fleet. This event celebrates the fishermen and their way of life, and honors those fishermen who have been lost. Area fishermen established the Blessing in 1954, influenced by similar events in Europe. Strong religious overtones and elements of Portuguese culture characterize the two-day festival, which takes place at the end of July. The two days have a very different character. Saturday is a day of celebration, offering an evening of food, beer, music, and dancing at the Town Dock, against the colorful backdrop of the many decorated boats.

Sunday is a more solemn day. It begins with a special fishermen's mass at St. Mary's Church in Stonington, where the altar is specially decorated for the occasion. Later, a parade winds through the streets of the village. Portuguese music and dancers in traditional costume provide a colorful highlight to the parade. The region's Catholic Bishop then presides over a ceremony at the fishermen's memorial, followed by the actual blessing of the fishing boats. The Bishop takes his place on one of the boats tied near the end of the dock. A procession of decorated boats then passes by the Bishop's position, and he blesses each boat in turn. The boats then proceed slowly out past the harbor's breakwater, where they form a wide circle. Here, members of a family that has lost relatives place a memorial wreath in the water.

A number of the fishing families eagerly look forward to the Blessing each year, and some take a very active role in its organization and management. The Blessing unites and reunites the fishing community and is very much a family event. Many people travel considerable distances to return to the area and visit with relatives and old friends. The event also brings together the community as a whole for the weekend. Although the fishing families are the most active participants, many other area residents and tourists observe or participate in the Blessing.

"It is a religious ceremony that I think we all need. Anytime we get a little blessing, we are going to take it. It is good festivity, where a lot of the fishermen, not all the fishermen, but a lot of fishermen get together and join in and help out and get this thing going. It also goes way back in my family as well. My grandfather was a good part of that. I've even got one of his trophies on the wall over there, that he won first place for the best dragger. In those days there were a lot of boats. You see pictures of them on postcards, there must have been 20-some, 30-some draggers, and they were all decorated. They made a big deal of it back then. I think a lot more then than now.

Of course, now I think we are trying to keep the tradition going and it is a struggle to keep it going. But I am the co-chairman of it, so I'm really involved in it very much. I've won quite a few trophies from it. We take it to heart quite a bit. A lot of people don't. My mother, she does her fried dough down there. She is probably the second-biggest benefactor down there for raising money for the Blessing of the Fleet. It's just something that we do. It's part of our life, part of the family life, tradition of fishing. If I was to give up fishing, I think that it would go away. The Blessing of the Fleet part would just fizzle away. Maybe it might work the other way to. Maybe if the Blessing of the Fleet went away, maybe the fishing would go away too. I don't know.

Tim Medeiros

It's in memory of all deceased fishermen, and it's asking for an abundance of fish. St. Pete is our patron saint. So that's the purpose of it. It's a solemn event, and it's also a happy event. There's a celebration and a solemn part.

The Blessing itself, I never ran it or anything. Then one year they did ask me to and I did. I tried it. I don't know, I kind of like being a part of it. I believe in it, and we have a lot of help. It's a satisfactory feeling, really, to do it and be successful and I just believe in the purpose of it. We've got 31 names down there, I believe, on the stone [monument]. People who have died at sea, and I know the biggest part of them. Some I grew up with as kids; we played together. From a drowning, one of my best friends fell off a mast. I just like to be a part of it, so my heart and soul goes with that, believe me.

Arthur Medeiros

It means a lot, because Sunday they do pay tribute to the people who lost their lives at sea. I had an uncle die of a heart attack in Watch Hill Bend. Right over the wheel. I had another uncle drown right off of Block Island. And I had another uncle fell out of a mast. The one that drowned was Albert. He was 19 when he drowned, in 1946, I think, or 1943. And my father jumped in after him, couldn't reach him. And there was three brothers fishing on the same boat when it happened. So they took it kind of tough."

Al Maderia

Blessing of the Fleet, Sunday scenes.

"And the other one was Arthur. He was the firecracker, they used to call him. And he was fishing on a boat in New Bedford, swordfishing, and he was up in the topmast looking for swordfish. He wasn't harnessed in–reason being that a friend of his was harnessed in and he fell out of the mast and the harness broke his back and he was in a wheelchair all his life. So he always swore that if anything ever happened, he just, he didn't want to be that way. When he was up there, I guess the mast let go. It wasn't his fault. When he fell he kept trying to push overboard but the boat was turning and he landed on the hatch. Killed him–29 years old.

And my uncle Manny was 60–58 or 59. They were setting. And my father was on the boat then, too. So he saw two of them die. They were setting in, and in the old days they didn't have all the [net] reels. They made the turn and you ran all your gear out. They kept noticing the boat made an extra turn. They went over, he was slumped over. He had a massive heart attack. Died right there. It's tough, you know. But I think that the Blessing is good. Pays that tribute. Somebody has to pay tribute.

Al Maderia

We never used to charge at the gate, but I think that the dollar or the two dollars they charge is appropriate. It's for a good cause, to promote it for the following year to come, to make sure that the tradition is carried on. It's a worthwhile thing. I'm one of the organizers now. Years ago, when I was younger, I lost an uncle and a cousin to a fishing accident, and it kind of started meaning something more. Because that's what it's all about, you're honoring your fishermen lost at sea. Giving thanks for a good season. You know, a time to remember. And I lost another cousin since then.

Mike Grimshaw

I help Arthur out quite a bit with it. I think it's a great event. It's just a time where most of the draggers, most of the lobster boats, they stop and just remember the guys we have lost at sea. I know you hear a lot about the Saturday night. Of course, now, we know all about the drinking laws and stuff, but it's just a fund-raising event, to put on Sunday, actually. But the religious part of it on Sunday is great. Just one day you're putting aside for these guys, you know? I'll do everything I can, as long as I can, for that purpose, definitely.

The families. We have people that have lost their brothers, or sons. They're the ones that throw the broken anchor overboard. And a couple of the fishermen, who died at home, their wives or family put the wreaths on the memorial on the end of the dock that Sunday. We get them all involved in it. It's quite a thing. It's a good thing.

John Rita"

Altar decorations, Blessing of the Fleet.

"

I've been working with the Blessing since I can remember. We always decorated my dad's boat. Then I got really involved about five years ago. I'm the secretary-treasurer for the Blessing. And I've been decorating St. Peter, I would say for the last six years, with my sisters. I love it. I love the Blessing. It's a lot of work, but I like it when Sunday comes and everything you've done gets put together and it comes out really good. It's sad when it rains, but still, it's there, and you know what it's for.

My oldest one marches pulling St. Peter. And my daughter walks with the dory that carries the small children. So she kind of watches. I used to do that and I stepped aside, let the younger ones do it. Actually I do some selling for the Blessing. I sell hats and different things directly for the Blessing. All the profits go right to the Blessing.

Ann Rita

I've been to every Blessing over the last 23 years. And it's such an important thing for the town. That and the Thanksgiving Day game between Stonington High School and Westerly High School. It's the only time you really catch up with everyone in town. They all show up. And it's a very friendly atmosphere, and especially on a Saturday night. It's the one time, now, being four years out of high school, I can see everybody, and I know they'll all be there.

And then, of course, Sunday is, especially for a fisherman and a fisherman's family. It's a very somber time. You remember the people who died at sea, and I've known some of them, my father knew most of them from the port. And I go to the Fisherman's Mass every year. And I just think it's the best local tradition that we have in the Borough. And it's nice to see such an important time, as far as religion goes, and in the social framework of the fishermen, celebrated by the town, and celebrated by the tourists. And it's really good. Every Blessing has its own special memory for me. I've always been able to go out on the flagship, and meet the Bishop, and see everything. It's really something.

Michael Medeiros

It does mean a lot to us, the Blessing of the Fleet. It really does.

Patty Banks

I feel a lot better when I come away from it. One thing I never want to forget, you know, what happened. And that day helps not to forget it. To me it's like paying a tribute to my son. That's why we do the flowers and stuff over there. Hopefully, he's looking down on us when we do that and he's saying, "My family still remembers me."

Al Banks

"

Family Traditions

Many of the lobstermen and fishermen of Stonington grew up in fishing families. Their fathers and other relatives worked as fishermen, and it was natural for them, as children, to spend time at the dock and around the boats. Many began fishing or lobstering at a young age. They were anxious to go out and experience a way of life familiar to others in their family. They understood that the older men were proud of their work. The boys and young men learned their trade from older relatives, and they also experienced the support of their mothers, grandmothers, and other women in their extended families. Many of the fishing families were Portuguese, and Old World traditions, including religious traditions, reinforced the fishing lifestyle.

Despite a strong heritage, family traditions of fishing are in jeopardy. Most young men are not following their fathers to the boats. Several factors, including an industry facing an uncertain future, are leading them away from fishing and into other careers. In many fishing families there is an impending break in tradition. For the first time in several generations, young men are not choosing the work of their fathers and grandfathers.

Between the piers, Town Dock.

"My family lived in the Stonington area all my life, and both sides of my family, both mother and father, were very active in the fishing business, especially on my mother's side. My grandfather, especially, came from the Azores in Portugal when he was a young lad. He already had family over here, and he was one of the main characters in getting the fishing fleet to what it is today. My father's side, they were in town but not so active in the fishing business; it was mostly on my mother's side. On my mother's side, all were lobstermen and fishermen, and most of them are not here anymore.

I got involved with my grandfather when I was about 12 years old. My grandfather gave up fishing on a dragger. He had his own dragger and then he sold it. He was getting kind of old for that. So he wanted to go lobstering, and he came to me and he asked if I would go lobstering with him in the summertime. I was very excited, and that's how I started. Just working summers with him, and I got to be around the docks and things.

Of course, my mother didn't like it too much. She was brought up in the tough days down there, when most of the guys, when they came in they went to the local pubs. I guess there used to be about nine pubs in Stonington, and I think they spent most of their time and money there. And the language barrier always was a little rough. She liked me to work for my grandfather, but when I grew up and got out of school she wanted me to take on other practices, which I did at first, but I went back.

Most of the men that I knew, the guys that I grew up with, I respected them and they were all honest men, and they taught me a lot. Yes, every summer I had to work with my grandfather, which meant that sports were out of the question, and anything else for that matter: playing, going to the beach. Once I committed myself, I was there. I had felt kind of stuck there for a while, and I wanted to be with my pals. I was a kid, a teenager growing up, and I had to work with a grumpy old man who could hardly even say my name. He had a Portuguese accent. You don't appreciate things like that when you are 13, 14, 15 years old. Later on in life, when they aren't here anymore, then you say, Gee, the things that that man could have taught me and the things that he did teach me that you took for granted back then."

Tim Medeiros

Susan & Frances, Blessing of the Fleet.

"

It was just get up at three in the morning. He would call me up "Timmy, get up." Boom! Down to the dock, all day long, he didn't have to do anything, I'd to be right with him every step of the way. And we even got into, at one point, when I got a little older, I was down helping him build lobster pots, and paint buoys, and things like this. I even got a credit from high school. That was probably one point of it that I enjoyed; I used to get out of high school at noontime to go down and help my grandfather out. He ended up giving me his boat when he got to the point of age where he couldn't do anything anymore. He gave me the boat, and I started on my own lobstering.

Tim Medeiros

I was born in Murtosa, Portugal, in 1934, January 13. Yes, it's on the mainland. I would say a couple hundred miles north of Lisbon. It's a little fishing community. Fishing and farming. That's what they did up there. I came here as a very young baby, about a year, sixteen months old, something like that. It was after Depression times. My recollection of, or from what my father tells me, and my mother, it was my grandfather's wish that his sons emigrate from Portugal. And they worked towards that end every year. They financed one son to come to this country. And my father came here after marrying my mother, and worked for the U.S. Rubber Company, or Uniroyal, in Naugatuck, Connecticut. And in the meantime, I was born while he was here. And I still have the letter that was written to officials in Portugal asking them to allow me to emigrate, because it wasn't as easy as it is now.

About 1944, after a few years of working in the factories, he didn't like it. And he was invited by a friend of his, Alfred Rubello, who was a fisherman from a town just south of us. They knew each other, and invited him to come down here and fish. They needed crews, and he had more than one boat that was looking for crews.

Of course, back then Portuguese fishermen were in demand because they were taught the basics that most people have to learn after they go fishing. These people were taught this as young men. When they're young. They started with their parents. None of this go play football, or baseball, or tennis, or whatever. You came home from school, if there was a school, and you help your parents survive. So, these people knew their business, their jobs, long before they even came here. They came here as fishermen, which was considered an art in the old country. It was something that you didn't learn in school, but it took a talent to know it. You had to have a knowledge, and this knowledge was already in these people.

Joe Rendeiro

"

Joe Rendeiro.

"So, of course, he came over here and started fishing, with Mr. Rubello, Alfred Rubello. And he later bought his first boat from Mr. Rubello. The beginning of my fishing career I think started when I was in the seventh grade at the Borough School. I could look out the windows and watch the fishing boats come and go. And I had no desire to be in school. I always wanted to be a fisherman.

There was nothing I wanted to be other than a fisherman. It was a good job. It was an honorable job. We were looked at as respectable people. We made money. We spent money freely. Some of the people, some of the younger guys, I guess, spent it foolishly. Stonington at that time had four or five barrooms, and it was a going town. And, of course, there were fishermen like my father that saved their money and invested in the business with another boat, and stuff like that. You know, thought about the future.

But Stonington was basically a fishing town. So, when I was a sophomore in high school and reached the age of 16, I decided I was going to go fishing. So, I got a job with Nat Culver. It didn't last long because Nat was an old man. My father objected to me going fishing. Basically, he wanted me to stay in school. So, he come home one day, and he says, "You want to go fishing?" He says to my mother, he says, "Rosa, you fix this boy up some clothes." Now, I'm 16 years old. So, I went fishing with my father.

And I can remember my first experience. One of the early experiences. And it was a wake up time for me, you know? And he was a hard taskmaster. But knowing what I know now, I can appreciate why he did the things he did. We ripped a net one day. And it was cold. We were fishing for herring. But anyway, we ripped this net. There was four men in a boat. All of them were mending on the net, and I was watching because I didn't know how to mend. But in the meantime, I had my hands in my pockets, see? And there was a lot of work to be done, but my hands were in my pockets. My father never said anything to me. Well, that night we got home and no matter what time we got home, that's when we ate supper. We all sat down to supper together. And without looking up from his food, from his dinner, my father says to my mother, says, "Rosa, I want you to sew every pocket that boy has, sew it up." At that time I got the message, you know? When there's work to do, you don't stick your hands in your pockets. I tried to relay that to a lot of the people I have in my crews, and it's tough to do.

Joe Rendeiro"

Mike, Bill, and Joe Bomster (L-R).

"

He made me work hard. But in the meantime, I learned my profession from him. He paid me in accordance to what I could do. Didn't make any difference, I knew I was doing as much as anybody else would do. But in order to push me to learn more, he never paid me unless I learned. I learned how to splice, and I learned how to mend, and I learned how to tie knots. I learned dead reckoning, navigation. That's what they did years ago. Because we didn't have the electronics we have today. How to use a sounding machine, you know, to tell where you are. Things of that nature. And that's how it all started.

Sam Roderick was one hell of a fisherman. I learned a lot from Sam Roderick. I got a lot of help from the Roderick family. Georgie Roderick, who died a short time after that. Billy Roderick, who recently died, was like my teacher. These people, when they talked, I would learn from them. I'd sit in the foc's'le with a bunch of fishermen, talking on a stormy day, and they would tell things, and I'd pick up information from their conversations on fishing grounds, how to rig nets, what to do. Back then I didn't know too much about that. So, whenever I needed to know something, I would ask them. And they would tell me. They would teach me. Most of this information they had, they gave freely. It was something that was done back then.

Joe Rendeiro

My mother's side of the family, all her brothers were fishermen, and my grandfather was a fisherman and a lobsterman. And my great uncles on my mother's side are all fishermen. The DeBraggas and the Rodericks. Her mother was a Roderick. I guess there were 13 brothers and sisters, and all the brothers were draggermen.

Mike Grimshaw

If you had heroes or role models when I was a kid, fishermen were my role models.

Joe Rendeiro

My father was a commercial fisherman for 29 years. He used to take me with him fishing in the summertime. I'd hear him get up and stuff. I'd be awake. He'd say, "You want to go?" I couldn't wait. I used to run right downstairs, get dressed, and go. Ever since then, that's what I wanted to be, and here I am today.

John Rita

"

Nathan Williams.

"

The fishermen I've known over the years, and I've heard the stories about my great uncles and all that, and they were all Portuguese. And I've found that the boats can change, and the fishing conditions can change, but the people really don't. I think if you took my Uncle Danny today, and put him on a boat, he'd be the exact same type of fishermen as he was when my father started fishing with him in the forties. And I think that has a lot to do with the closeness of Portuguese families. It's getting away from that now, because now we're second- and third-generation Americans, but it used to be that Sunday was the day that you went to the oldest grandmother's house. And you went there and had a nice big Portuguese dinner, and the whole family came. And I think that's what's kept the feeling of community with the fishermen going over the years. They all come from the same backgrounds, and they all had relatives that were fishermen. And fishing was a great business to get into. There was, there still is a lot of support within the Portuguese community for fishermen, and for the life they choose. A lot of support.

Michael Medeiros

My son is doing it now. My son worked with me all these years, and he wanted to do it himself. So he's doing it today. He's doing a great job. Great job. While he's fishing I take care of everything on the dock. That's my job. It's a business, but it's a family business. And now he's got his son that goes with him to help him pick lobsters. He's ten. And once in a while one of his other sons goes with him, too. It's a regular tradition, doing it just the way I did it.

Manny Maderia

I never wanted to be a fisherman. I admired it, and especially when I went to college, I really appreciate the life my father led, and what he had given me as far as his attitude. But I always felt that I didn't really want to do it. I guess it was just something that I liked to know about, without ever considering doing. I have some cousins, their fathers are fishermen, and all of them have gone through a stage where all they wanted to be was fishermen. And for some reason that never struck me. I wanted to be a baseball player.

Michael Medeiros

"

Manny Maderia (L) and Richie Maderia.

"

I was lucky enough to get to know my father very well, and grow to like him as a person, in addition to as a father. And it's very close. There are some days without barely saying a word to each other, and just, oh, nod here, and a grunt there to get through the day. And other days you just have someone to talk to all day long. You learn a lot about somebody being cooped up with them all day long. I know my father said the same about me. He didn't really know me before I was a fisherman. And I didn't know him either. We got to know each other, good and bad. The boat really promotes that.

Michael Medeiros

My son worked for me for two years. He is not a fisherman, he doesn't like the hours for one thing. I'm not fond of the hours myself, but he didn't want to do it. He did it for two years, and I am surprised he did. He was a good man on the boat. But he said "bye" and that was it. I tried to encourage him a little bit. I tried to teach him things, but he just didn't have the interest. He just didn't have it. I was different. When I was 12, 13 years old, I wanted to know why this did that and that did that, and I could see right away that he didn't have that. He never asked any questions.

Tim Medeiros

All the downtime. You're out there for 12- or 13-hour days, and six or seven hours you might not be doing anything. And there were the soap operas to watch on TV, and there was no place to go, and nothing really to do. And, if you're not working, and you've already seen it, you don't really appreciate the downtime. You wish something were happening all the time. I used to think it was a real boring life, because you'd go out and it'd be three or four hours before anything happened, before any fish came on deck. You'd be steaming out and setting the net, and towing the net, and waiting. And there was nothing to do except, you know, watch "Good Morning, America" and take a nap.

Michael Medeiros

I went out lobstering when I was younger, with my dad, before I started working, and I liked it. I liked the water. It gives you a sense of freedom. It really does. You're on your own. And so I understand how he [John] feels when he's out there. Don't get me wrong, I do worry. I worry all the time, but you put it aside. We have a good life. I wouldn't change it.

Ann Rita

"

John Rita.

George McCagg (L) and Art Medeiros.

Economics
and the Business of Fishing

John Rita (L) and John Grimshaw.

Economic Aspects of Fishing

Lobster.

The economic aspects of the fishing industry present a challenge that can be as difficult for the fishermen to confront as stormy weather. The prevalence of lobsters and target fish species varies, and prices fluctuate depending on scarcity and season. The price markup of fish, from the boat to the store, is dramatic. A fishermen may receive $ 1.50 per pound for fish that will be sold in a local market for $ 11.99 per pound. Costs steadily escalate for fishermen who must meet the expenses of boats and equipment, maintenance, vessel insurance, health insurance, association dues, safety equipment, fuel, ice, repairs, and other goods and services. Increasing costs and unpredictable income make it difficult for many fishermen to continue in the industry.

"

There is no way today you can let stuff lay, just sit there idle. The cost, the insurance. is unbelievable: $50,000 a year. It's a $1,000 a week just to insure it. That's PI and hull–personal injury, somebody gets hurt on the boat, big dollars. So you've got to be rolling all the time. You've got your mortgage, and you know, you're talking a $500,000 vessel. And maintenance on the motors. Nobody works for under $50.00 an hour any more and so you've gotta keep 'em rolling all the time. They're definitely work machines.

Jim Allyn

We're trying to help the fishermen. That's our whole purpose of being here. And you want the best prices a fisherman can get. And hopefully competition is helping. It's healthy, that's the American way: Capitalism. They all make jokes about the fish buyers in New York. They say they all sit down and have coffee in the morning and set the price.

Well, they're independent, you know that. That's why they're fishermen. They certainly are not in it for the money. So, they can go anyplace they want. Like I've heard time and time again, this boat's got a propeller, this boat could go anyplace. And they do. If they don't like the price here, they'll go to Newport, they'll go to New Bedford, they'll go to Point Judith, go to Long Island. They're not tied to these buyers even though these are their home-port buyers. It's nicer to come home and take out your fish here and get a fair price for it. But, if they don't feel like they're getting a fair price, they go someplace else.

The buyers set the price, the fisherman doesn't set the price. Years ago, there was a New Bedford auction every morning that set the price. And that was, supposedly, roughly what the fish was worth on that day. But it's so inaccurate. And a lot of boats wouldn't go under the auction. They wouldn't go on the board. Say a guy had a trip of codfish, and the buyer wanted the codfish. And say he had 1,000 pounds of yellowtails, or 2,000 pounds of yellowtails. He might be the only guy on the board that day. They guy might pay $2.00 for the yellowtail in order to get the codfish for 60 cents. See what I mean? So, here you'd see the New Bedford auction price of $2.00 for yellowtails when they're only worth a buck. So, it wasn't an accurate price.

We've had different buyers here that used to offer what they called a road price. Buy the yellowtails here and truck them back to New Bedford to get cut. So, they'd pay a nickel under the New Bedford board, or dime under, or whatever. Other than that, the price is set down in Fulton Fish Market. But it's very imperfect. It's supply and demand, but it's a very imperfect system. So, you don't know what you're going to get for your fish until you get the return.

Dick Bardwell

"

Bob Rinaldi.

"

You've got to work with a buyer, too. You've got to give him a good product. You've got to try to bring it in when he needs it, and let him know you're coming. There's a lot of different things. The more communication between the boat and the buyer, the better off it is for both of them. And there are different places they can go with their fish, too. Sometimes a buyer might have a customer that needs fish desperately. And he'd pay more for it, because he needs it. So, that guy can give the boat more. It's very imperfect.

Normally, they're within pennies of each other. Within nine, ten, fifteen cents of each other, normally. In other words, they should be. Basically, most of the fish goes to Fulton, and they pay the same price for the fish. So, it's what the buyer's going to take, what his costs are for the ice, the labor, the box, the trucking.

And his profit. Say the fish goes to New York. If you're talking 100,000 pounds of squid, and you've taken it out in eight hours, you can certainly work on a lot smaller margin than if you're talking a couple hundred pounds of flounder. If you did five cents on 100,000 [pounds], that's $5,000. That's a nice profit. But if you take five cents on three hundred pounds of flounder, that's not much profit at all. That's $15.00

Dick Bardwell

We do have the choice, and we also have the choice of shipping our fish through them. We can ship them to any fish buyer. We can ship them to Point Judith, we can ship them to New York, we can ship them to Philadelphia. We just pay them a packing fee.

It's not new that we have two buyers, it is just that we were without two buyers for a while, and we felt the crunch, at a very critical time last spring when we had our run of fish. It is the best run of the year for us "inshore draggers," we call ourselves, the day boats. We kind of thrive on that two-month span that is right around Memorial Day, where we catch the most fish that we catch all year long. And the only buyer in Stonington kind of put it to us, saying it mildly. We didn't make the money we should have made. And a few of us did change. You can jump back and forth. There is no hard feelings, not with the buyer anyway. You need a competitive edge, and that's what that's all about.

Tim Medeiros

Right now I'm selling down here in Stonington, but I do have a buyer for my scallops. I sell directly to New Bedford. I just truck them up there. Fish and stuff like that I deal locally here with the local fish buyers. And they buy it and do whatever they've got to do. Like the squid, the butterfish, all that kind of stuff, scup, most of that stuff goes down to Jersey, down that way. New York gets a lot of it, Fulton Market. That kind of stuff, the soft stuff seems to go to the west, down New York way. The flat stuff, the stuff you cut, goes up to New Bedford.

"

Jim Allyn

Stonington Fillet interior.

"We don't weigh everything on our boat, naturally. We could but we don't. We have an idea of what we've caught every day. We know probably within 40 or 50 pounds of what we've got. They take it out, if they don't call it out right then they'll put it on a pallet, tag it, and they'll do it later on in the day, or the next day. Each day they will make a tally slip up, so many of this, so much of that, and they put the name of your boat on top of it. If they are calling right then and there, you can get a slip right from them, right when they are done. I usually don't wait around. We haven't had too many problems. Every now and then they'll miss something. Usually you just say, "Look, I had something you didn't have." They will look around, they can find it, or take your word for it and know that you're honest enough. And the prices are on a daily basis. They vary day to day. If we take out today, we'll get tomorrow's price, because they have to know what the market did. We come in at four, or five, or six o'clock at night, they don't know what the next day's price is. That is what they base it on. That is how that works.

We constantly want to know what we are getting. It almost makes you want to go fishing or not go fishing. There have been times when there have been plenty of fish, but we just didn't go out because we weren't getting enough money for them. It wasn't worth it. It's worth it, but it's a shame to give them away for those prices sometimes. Just let them go, let them breed. But we watch it very closely, yes.

You've got to ask. You have to go in the office, and say, "What is the price for fish?" If you are not a fish buyer, or fisherman, or owning a fishing boat, they might just tell you to go elsewhere and do something else.

In my case it is usually every four days, I have to fill up my tanks. But it is only deducted on the end of the trip. We get the settlement check from the fish buyer, get the tally from the dock, how much ice and fuel we used for the week, and that comes right off first. That is the first expense. There is no other unless you have a grub order. That's it. Take that away, take your boat share, and whatever is left, you split with your crew and that is your pay. Like it or not.

The boat share, I would say an average is usually 50 percent. Well what happens is it is a 50/50 deal, if you've got two people on the boat, like myself and the man with me. We split the other 50 percent, so he gets 25, I get 25. If there's three men on the boat, it would be three ways that way. And so on and so forth.

Tim Medeiros"

Chet Murray filleting a fish.

"

Economics tell us what we're going to do. Like a good example would be we're dragging right now. But if the price falls out and the amount of fish falls out, why, economics will say to us, "you better go scalloping". So, we will. And we pride ourselves on this versatility. Not everybody has it. We happen to have it. So, we're very fortunate. And it didn't come easy. It's a lot of expense involved to learn both sides of the coin.

Walter Allyn

Fuel's probably $400 or $500 a week with the oil changes, with that kind of stuff. Bait is about $1,200 to $1,500 a week. Sometimes it's a little more, depending if I buy ahead. But we use about 200 to 250 bushels of bait a week fishing that much gear. If we buy local bait, it's $5.00 a bushel, plus your salt. If you buy the menhaden, it's $30.00 a barrel or $32.00 a barrel sometimes.

Mike Grimshaw

It's tough. It's tough to keep it all together like this situation we just ran into. The trip before we came back, we had caught a rock in the net and it must have been as big as a car and took our whole net. I mean, $10,000 worth of gear gone in less than two minutes. Two minutes. We had it up to the boat and, boom, it was gone. Ten grand. Gone. It's something you have to pay for. Insurance doesn't cover it unless it's over ten grand. The deductible's ten grand. So, that was that. You have to have enough gear, so you have to build another net. So we just built another net. That wasn't too bad, but we had to haul out for the tail shaft. That was bad. We just did the haul out, the bearings and whatnot. That was another ten grand. You got to keep up on them and they're expensive, you know. Tough business.

Phil Torres

And then the government keeps coming out with more safety things we've got to keep buying. But you can't go out and make the money, and they want you to buy all this stuff. You're saying, "How am I going to afford to buy this at X amount of thousands, when I'm cut back?" You can't. Something has to go. And if you start taking away from the boat, of course, you get back to the picture where you're not comfortable with what you're in. And any kind of weather, you're just, "Oh, boy, I should have done that, I didn't do this, I should have done this." But finances aren't there.

John Rita

When we could build a pot for less than $5.00, we were getting $2.50 for our lobsters. And now the pot costs $35.00 and they're still getting $2.50 for their lobsters. So you look at inflation of the materials, the costs of boats, the costs of the pots, the lobsters should be $25.00 a pound. But, of course, they aren't. Very few people do it, but it's real interesting to sit down and figure out just how much it costs you to catch a lobster. And if it costs you $1.75 to catch a lobster, and you're only getting $2.50 for it, it's not a very good business.

"

Dick Bardwell

Jeff Medeiros and lobster.

“

Years ago, we were getting $3.50 a pound in the summertime. That goes back 20 years ago. Today, in the summertime, you're looking at $2.50, $2.75, maybe $3.00 once in a while. Depending on the demand on a holiday, or something. The understanding is not there, of inflation, in this business. It's just gone the other way. Prices of all your materials have gone up, but the price of the lobsters has come the other way. That's hard. Hard to understand. Real hard.

Richie Maderia

General public has no idea whatsoever what we've gotta go through to catch fish. And then what kills me is I'll come in with a boatload of flounder or something. I'll get 50, 60 cents for 'em, and you go to the market and they're $7.99, $8.00 dollars a pound. And we get 40, 50, 60, 70, 80 cents.

I was scalloping and I looked up on Route 1 there, in that little fish market on the corner. Used to kill me. I'd come in, get $3.50, $4.00 a pound for scallops. And every time I'd come in, that next morning I see this great big sign out there in the front window. It'd say, “Sea scallops, fresh sea scallops for sale: $7.99 a pound.” They are my scallops, went from my boat, down the street maybe two miles to this guy's place and it's already doubled in price. Where's the justice here?

I mean here you are, the public, buying this stuff at this un-Godly amount of money, you know. And here we are working our butts off to catch it. And you know a lot of times you feel like you're not getting paid what you should. There's too many middlemen, now. Too many people in between, taking a little here, taking a little there.

Jim Allyn

I had a lady come over and just chew me out royally about two years ago. Saying that we were making all the money because she was paying $7.99 for a pound of flounder fillets. And I was getting upset. I told her, “Lady, if you think we make $7.99 a pound for each pound of that fish we're taking out, you're wrong.”

At the time we were making 60 cents a pound for the whole fish. It takes two point something pounds to make a pound of fillets. So it's only costing the guy a dollar something to make these fillets up. A dollar eighty even, say three pounds, yet we're making all the money? I said, “Lady, I can take you home, open my books up and show you what I pay for boat mortgage payment, insurance, fuel, ice, everything. And at that 60 cents a pound, we're making a living, but we're not getting rich.” And she's insisting that we made all the money. I said, “Well, look at my Mercedes down there.” At the time I had an eighty-four El Camino with a banged-up door. That's what I drive, I mean, you know, it's not what you think. The middleman makes most of the money in this business.

Al Maderia

”

David Angrisani (L) and Michael Brennan.

"

They don't like the high prices sometimes and they think that, "Yes, the fishermen must be doing really good." You go now, today, to the market and get fillets at $6.99 a pound or whatever it is. My husband may get a dollar something a pound. It's not the fishermen that are making the money, and so they work the hardest for the least. Basically, I would say anybody that's self employed has to work the hardest and that's what my husband is.

Ann Rita

Well, that's something in this business you've got to really plan. Like right now the boat's hauled out. We've been two weeks out of business now. Had to paint her up, do maintenance, go through the boat, sandblasting. All that, get the propeller reworked, the rudder reworked, all new bearings. Big job. Kind of bear with it. And in the winter, your trips are shorter, you get two, three, four days. You get a big blow, you run in with it.

Jim Allyn

You really have to look at the good times and make sure you're able to adjust to the bad times. I saved some money over the wintertime for summer. As it turns out, this particular month, I ran into a situation where I had scheduled to take off a week at the end of the month, and it turns out the boat had to be hauled out at the beginning of the month. So, we're just getting the boat back today. Which means that I missed a trip before my vacation trip that I was supposed to take off. Usually you want to just miss one trip, and that's that. If you miss one trip of monking or scalloping it's twenty days off. You figure five days in when you get in, ten days for the trip, and then another five days when those guys get in. So, I'm going to end up missing the whole month right out of my year, if I still want my scheduled time off which I have to have. Schedule that I made plans for it. It just turns out that I'm not going to be on the trip before that. You have to really be prepared for things like that to come up.

The summer's always lean. You're making longer trips for less money. The wintertime you always do better. You can make up to $500 a day in the wintertime. And in the summertime you can make $100 a day. Usually, you don't want to go out fishing for anything less than $100 a day. It's usually not worth it.

Phil Torres

If I made a lot of money, I put it in the bank, and that carries you over when you don't. If you own a boat, and if your engine blows a block or something, you've got to have a slush fund. Back then, it was $3,500 to fix that. Now, it's about $6,000. The engine, I think when she was new she cost $10,500. Now, they're $35,000.

Robert Berg

My grandmother always told me feast or famine, you know, and that's mostly what it is. You get your good months and you get your big trips, you've got to learn to salt a little bit of it away. Hang on to it a little bit, for the bad times.

Jim Allyn

"

Fishery Regulations and Restrictions

Looking astern onboard *Seafarer*.

The business of fishing, or the economics of fishing, have changed drastically in the past several decades. The fishing industry worldwide is in transition and, in many areas, serious decline. This is primarily due to depleted fish stocks and the increased regulation of the surviving stocks.

The fishermen acknowledge that protection of fish stocks is necessary, but they believe existing and proposed regulations are excessively severe. They feel that at least some years of fish scarcity are the results of natural cycles. They question the validity of the information base created by scientists and researchers and used by legislators and regulatory officials. Inconsistent and varying regulations from state to state are an added complication. On certain occasions, Connecticut fishermen have had to cease fishing because they met their quota, and then stand by as fishermen from other states caught the fish that Connecticut regulations were supposedly protecting.

The commercial fishing regulations are complex and frequently changing. When Mystic Seaport began its Stonington Fishing Oral History Project in 1993, the New England Fisheries Management Council had just implemented Amendment 7 to its fisheries management plan for the Northeast. Currently, Amendment 13 is about to take effect. This equals seven amendments in a 10-year period, indicating the frequent revisions to fishing regulations. The regulations implement closed areas, limited entry of new boats to the fishing industry, specified numbers of fishing days, and catch limitations on various species. Keeping up with the regulations is a time-consuming process, but it is an essential part of a fishermen's work today. That matter becomes even more complicated for Stonington's day boats and lobster boats, because their fishing grounds include the waters of three different states. They must know their federal regulations, plus the state regulations of Connecticut, Rhode Island, and New York. The regulations can also result in added expenses. In some cases, the changes have made it necessary for the fishermen to replace expensive gear, such as nets, when regulations call for larger mesh sizes to let more juvenile fish escape.

"

I don't know what the answer is. Obviously, we've got to have regulations, but it's hard to determine what are the right regulations.

Dick Bardwell

Like I said, the regulations still haven't kicked in. I think next month they are going to start going into effect, where you can only fish so many days, got to use a certain size mesh. There is nothing there now to regulate that we can see. We're not saying that we don't need regulations, but it is really going to hurt.

They are late, they are a little late. And they are a little extreme. It is probably what they have to do. I don't know; I'm not a scientist. We've seen lulls in fishing before, and they have come back. I've heard of even worse times than now, but it has always come back. Mother Nature has a way of doing things. I don't think that is going to be the case now. I don't know. A lot of people already have gone down, and there's going to be more to follow.

Tim Medeiros

Right now, the government's up in arms. You know, you've heard of all that. Regulations and rules. It's getting tough, they're really getting tough, but something's got to get done. You can't just keep beating away on a resource and expect it to last forever. You know, you've got to make some changes.

But I think what the government's gonna get more into, I really believe, we do have to go with a limited entry. A lot of people are dead against that. I feel that the boats are so big and so strong and so powerful today and there's just so many of them, that there's no way the resource's gonna keep up with us. It's like drilling oil. I mean you tap the well so many times, pretty soon it's gonna be dry, right?

It's just not the way this country's run. And they're gonna fight you all the way. But I think that's the only answer because I've seem 'em, I've seen it time and time again. The government coming up with regulated mesh sizes, closed areas, and all of that stuff, and it just isn't working. It is not working. I'm there every day, I see it. And I'm a young guy and I've got a long way to go in this business. You know, you've gotta bite the bullet somewhere here. Everybody does. Gonna have to take a reduction.

Jim Allyn

I'm not saying the government should subsidize them, but they've got to do something. It can't be all take, take, take. It's not like a farmer where you own the land. You don't own the ocean, but you've got an investment. In your boat, your learning, what you've done to get this. And it's really got a value. And to just take it away, by telling them you can't go fishing, is not right.

Dick Bardwell

"

Arthur Medeiros mending a net

"

They've got some good laws out now. They have some great laws out. Size of the fish, and the mesh, and everything. But I think it's too late. The damage's been done. Now they're trying to bring it back, and it's not going to be easy.

Manny Maderia

The way they're doing it now, you can't make a move without breaking the law. No matter what you do. You're out fishing, they change the law. It's absolutely asinine, and they're making such rules and regulations on what you have to have on a boat, I mean they just passed a law that you've got to have CPR training, for crying out loud, on a boat.

Charlie Fellows

Oh, that's the other reason I got out. They can't run the government. When they start telling you how to run the fishing business. The first time they had it, they came out with regulations, the guy who was the head of it, they had to show him a picture of a codfish, and he was making the regulations. He didn't even know what it looked like. All he was using is data, data, data. From what? The data was antique.

Robert Berg

Rules and regulations, modern-day rules and regulations from National Marine Fisheries and state and other things, you've read in the newspapers how we bond together. Fishermen up and down the coast are bonding together. The federal government was sued by Concerned Citizens for Conservation about us exploiting the natural resource belonging to the public. And they won. And that's where all these rules and regulations come about. I don't think they're all well-founded. I know they're not all well-founded. But people are trying to do the best they can. And we're trying to do the best we can. But we won't be put under. No rule or regulation is going to put a fisherman under, if he can help it.

Walter Allyn

It seems like every time they've made a change in the past few years, we've actually lost money. We have, there's no question about it. And I'm not just talking about the federal government; I'm talking about state, state waters. And when they started off with one size [of mesh] and going to another size and another size, and every time they do it, it was supposed to help out and it didn't, and they'd just take it out of our pockets, without putting anything back in it.

Tim Medeiros

We have Connecticut game wardens checking us either when we come into Connecticut waters if we're fishing in there, or we have dockside inspections by Connecticut game wardens or federal game wardens. And we also get boarded by the Coast Guard when we're in state waters or in federal waters.

Mike Grimshaw

"

Fishermen's Memorial.

"They look at your lobsters and how cold it is, or how hot. You can't take every one out of the tank, it's too cold or it's too hot. We'll lose them one way or the other, if it's too hot they'll die, if it's too cold you take them out of the tank they'll flash-freeze and lose claws and stuff if it's really cold. So, they kind of look at a couple of them just to make sure they're legal. And pull out all your paperwork, make sure you got all your EPIRB [Emergency Position-Indicating Radio Beacon] and your life preservers, make sure you have all your licenses, registrations, radio licenses, radar licenses, EPIRB licenses. I mean, you need to go fishing nowadays with a briefcase, not with a gaff hook and a pair of boots.

Biggest thing is, they need some accurate data. That's one of the biggest things. Connecticut has one step on that, our end of it, because we have logbooks recording our history and what's going on, how many pots we haul, how many days we fish, where we're fishing them at. We're one step up on almost the whole East Coast because of that. As to what's going on, some of the data they're trying to cram down our throats as being the best scientific data available–I love the phrase–is outdated and kind of sketchy. And then, of course, we have the "We put it into our model" –another one I love–and "we're overfished by x percent." Well, why do we keep having these record years? This year we had the biggest run as far as sizewise that we've had in a lot of years. Productwise it's big, enormous. Seemed like some days the smallest I had was a pound and a half. But that's one of the biggest issues is the scientific data they put forth. The fishermen, everybody's got an opinion. Some guys are trying to make their opinion, their firsthand experience knowledgeable to these scientific groups. And they don't want to hear it because it doesn't fit in to their scenario and their model of what's going on. Until they get those issues resolved then there's going to be conflict.

Mike Grimshaw

I don't know, these guys in Washington, where they get all their information, but wherever they get it, it's damned poor information, in my estimation.

George Berg

It could work out so well, they are basic plans but they don't want to listen to us. We're dumb, we don't know nothing. We're out there everyday, but supposedly we don't see what's going on.

I love the profession, but I don't like the way it's turning. I don't like to be regulated. When you know that the regulations are so off the wall, that hurts. I think they go to extremes. Too much. You don't mind if the regulations are made by people who know what they're talking about. When you've got people who've never done it, probably never even set foot on a fishing boat, I don't think that's fair. I don't think it's right."

Al Maderia

Nathan Williams measuring a lobster.

"

If you're fishing federal waters and you're off-loading in more than one state, you have to be aware of all the federal regulations, their reporting requirements as far as logbooks and things. And each state you go into, their licensing, their laws, which can be different from state to state, what their quotas are. How many pounds of fluke you can have on board in Rhode Island and off-load, compared to Connecticut, or New York, or Massachusetts, depending on the port you come into. That type of thing.

So I can appreciate what they're saying. It's a lot to keep up with. And I think they're trying to make it simpler. I think that the National Marine Fisheries Service and the states are realizing that it's becoming too complicated. And I know there's been a move on to try and get one reporting system, use the National Marine Fisheries Service reporting log and just have carbon copies, so to speak, and send them to the state you're in. Try and make it simpler that way. I don't know what the future holds as far as that, but I know that's been one of the big concerns that's been talked about, it's becoming too complicated. And there's a lot of equipment now, depending on what you're fishing for commercially. Whether you're fishing for scallops, whether you're fishing for tuna, or what have you. And there's regulations for them all.

Tom Brelsford

And it's a shame that we've got to catch them and we've got to throw them back overboard. And, you know, they're dead. And I can't find any rhyme or reason to why we've got to do that. We go 12 hours out to try to make a living, and they make us throw it overboard. And North Carolina, and all the Carolina boats come right in our backyard. They can fill the boats right up and take them home. Take all the fish home they want. But we can't go out here and bring them to Connecticut, or Rhode Island, or Massachusetts. The laws aren't the way they're supposed to be, I don't think.

Manny Soares

Can you put yourself in this position? You're in the middle of the Atlantic Ocean fishing on the continental shelf. On your port side there's a man from Rhode Island. On your starboard side there's a man from Massachusetts. On your stern there's a man from New York. And they can all catch fluke and bring them home. And you can't. So, what does that tell you? Think about it.

Walter Allyn

Because we're so close in the Sound, you have to make sure exactly where you put your pot overboard. Boundaries, where you can fish. I mean, what state. "Oops, I'm in New York."

Mike Grimshaw

"

Manny Soares (L) and Kenny Santos.

"

I mean, I would say I get boarded probably three or four times a year. And last year they said if we had a dockside inspection, we wouldn't have that problem anymore, and I did get the dockside inspection and the dockside inspection is to have all your safety stuff done at the dock by the Coast Guard. And they give us a sticker. So, now, when they come alongside, they ask for the sticker, and they come aboard anyhow.

Manny Soares

We didn't have much choice. We didn't have any notice. We had met with the state the Monday before we left, and we came in on like a Thursday, and he said fishing as usual, go right out. So, we went out and got our limit, and came back and got arrested for it. We were made the example, and we were the home-port boats that were supposed to be awarded that amount of fish. And we fought, the year before, to get more fish. And this year the out-of-state boats, you know, Rhode Island, Massachusetts, brought their fish into [Stonington] after their quotas were full and filled our quotas.

Phil Torres

I'm not in agreement with 99 percent of the rules and regulations they come out with.

Walter Allyn

The way it used to be was if you had a lot of ambition, you made a lot of money. Now, it's not that way anymore. Because if you have a lot of ambition, you can't go out and catch what you want and bring it in. You know, if you knew more than the other guy, you would make more money than him. But in the wintertime, we're on limits: 3,000-pound limits, 5,000-pound limits. The guy who didn't know as much as you did, he can do the same thing as you can. You can't catch what you could catch.

Manny Soares

Well, you could wallpaper the wheelhouse with the rules and regulations, but you certainly can't remember them all. They're ridiculous. You know, some of them are really ridiculous. You know, you need some regulations, certainly. Of course, you do. But some of them. The people that make the rules have no idea what they're talking about. They ought to go out fishing and try it and maybe they'd know what was going on, and then, maybe they could make some rules that would be worthwhile.

Betty Fellows

I like to fish, and I don't like to throw good fish back, and you've got to throw a nice big fluke overboard, or a nice big flounder overboard, because it's against the law to bring them in. That kind of gets you down.

Manny Soares

"

Fish

Fish being off-loaded.

Fish and lobster are the key factors in the economics of the Stonington fishing industry. The primary species targeted by the Stonington fleet include lobster, scallops, flounder, fluke, scup, butterfish, whiting, and some cod. Markets have also been found for species that would have been considered trash fish in the past, including monkfish, skates, and squid.

Ultimately, it is the scarcity or abundance of target species that determines the earning potential and financial survival of the fishermen and lobstermen. Low populations generally lead to greater catch restrictions, a step intended to help restore fish stocks. Fish populations also seem to be influenced by natural cycles, although these trends are not fully understood. While there is considerable debate about the health of various fish stocks, it is certain that overfishing has been harmful to at least some species. Still, fishermen report the presence of some species in impressive and increasing numbers, suggesting that regulations have been helpful.

"

And there were days, my father was telling me, five people couldn't keep up with the fish you had on deck. From bow to stern, rail to rail, a foot deep with yellowtail flounder, and I think in six months I saw about three yellowtail flounder. It's really a shame.

Michael Medeiros

If you talk to the old-timers, as bad as fishing is right now, in 1953 or '54 it was that bad then and it got better. Now we weren't over-fishing then, we didn't have the technology and all the equipment then. And what was the excuse back then? It came back. Cycles.

Al Maderia

The fish stocks, I don't know. Things like haddock, I hope they'll come back. I don't know. yellowtails have always run in cycles, for the last 30 or 40 years. They talk about years where there were no yellowtails, and years where there were a lot of yellowtails. So, I'm not even sure that has too much to do with overfishing. It probably has. That's one of the variables, but we don't know.

Dick Bardwell

I've seen this before. I've been around since the mid-forties. I've seen the depletion of the yellowtail stock. I've seen them come back. I've seen the scallops disappear, I've seen them come back. Now, they're on a down side again. Any day now, fish may come back. This cycles thing the species go through.

Walter Allyn

And of course, we have cycles too. Fish do run in cycles. They definitely do. You know, water temperatures, I don't know exactly what causes it but they definitely do run in cycles. Back in the fifties my father says he can remember the days when you could tow out here off Watch Hill Beach, all day long for two, three baskets of fish. And that's the way it is today. But back in 1978, right through 1981, I guess was the all-time record high in yellowtail landings. Everywhere you went the ocean was alive with 'em. Now where'd they all go? We didn't catch them all. I don't believe it. I just don't believe it. You know, and just recently two or three years ago, I'd say '89, '88, we had a big run of small yellowtails. Nine-, ten-inch fish. We're required by law to keep them at thirteen, but these were all nine, ten, eleven fish and they were just everywhere. And we thought we were gonna have a big run of those fish the next year, and the things just disappeared as fast as they came. So I think they'll be back.

Jim Allyn

Some things are still like clockwork. Like the flounder. It doesn't last as long. There's not as many as there used to be, but they are still on time. The big surge. It seems like there is nothing, nothing, nothing, and bang! There they are. You could be fishing all around, and they are right in this one spot, and how in the heck did they get there. It seems like they come up from a hole in the bottom of the ocean floor somewhere. And maybe they do. I don't know, but it is pretty weird.

Tim Medeiros

"

Bobby Peterkin picking the deck on *Seafarer.*

"Skates, they've started to sell skates. Around here they use them just for lobster bait. But now they cut the wings out and they, I don't know what they make out of them. They eat them. Actually, I've seen them in the Stop & Shop market. Skate wings for sale.

Dick Bardwell

We try to concentrate on fluke, but we're also keeping squid, scup, and all that good stuff. Butterfish, we've got big markets now over in Japan. The Japanese buy a lot of our butterfish. Whiting. The Spanish now are buying whiting that we catch, that we always used to just throw away. There was no market for it in this country, but that's turning into a big thing too. The Spanish are buying them.

Jim Allyn

Yes, I agree we overfish a little bit in certain species. Last winter we had the fluke overfishing, if you remember reading about it in the paper. But we had more fluke last year than I've ever seen before. I had to call our vessel home after two and a half days. He had 7,000 pounds on the boat. Had to call him back.

Walter Allyn

Overfishing's easy to jump on, because you can see it. But pollution, we have no idea, really, what effect pollution's had on the fish stocks. Theoretically, we're getting better. I don't know whether we are or not. Everybody feels the Sound is cleaner. I don't know whether it really is, or not. It should be cleaner. Most of these towns have got sewage treatment plants now, that they didn't have 20 years ago. Don't have a lot of cottages and factories and stuff, pumping right into the ocean. I would think that would help the stocks. Nature has a way of replenishing itself, in spite of man. But if you destroy the habitat, that's much more serious than destroying the stocks. If you destroy the habitat, you've had it. So, I think, probably attacking from that end would be more beneficial in the long run for improving the stocks.

Dick Bardwell

I would say the groundfish, there aren't as many. Like the yellowtail, codfish, flounder. I would say they're depleted pretty good. The fluke I have to disagree. There's more fluke out there now than I saw in a long time.

Manny Soares

I think most of the fish is all overfished. Everywhere you go. That's my opinion of it. Everything is all overfished. Lobstering. I don't care, you name it, it's all overfished. The way I look at it, they're just cleaning that ocean right up. Just cleaning it right up.

Manny Maderia"

The Future of Stonington Fishing

Dressed for winter work.

Despite the challenges facing the fishermen of Stonington, the fleet seems to be faring generally well, although success varies from boat to boat. The scallop industry is prospering, providing impressive catches and bringing new scallop boats into the Stonington fleet. The lobster industry has experienced setbacks but seems to be holding its own, although it is cyclical. A slow season may be followed by a surprisingly good season. The off shore and inshore draggers are meeting with mixed success. Only about a dozen draggers now fish out of Stonington. This represents a significant reduction in a fleet that in past decades included 40 or more of these vessels. Some boats and crews are increasing their earnings by diversifying their catches and seeking markets for species that were previously considered trash fish, such as squid.

Declining fish stocks and increased regulation have driven some Stonington men away from fishing. While many members of the Stonington fishing community try to remain positive and optimistic, they are very concerned about an uncertain future.

"

Well if it goes where it sounds like it is going, it is going to drive a lot of people out of business. If you can't make it, you've got to get out, you have no choice. You've got to do something else. We're trying, we're struggling. We've refinanced everything again for probably the fourth time, hopefully the last. And that is just putting things off. I think I am in a good category, because of the size of the boat I have, because of my overhead, and they think a lot of these restrictions aren't going to affect me because of the size of my boat. So I may have a chance. But there still has to be some fish.

Tim Medeiros

I think people are going to keep fishing as long as they possibly can. I'm afraid the government is very much against the independent fisherman. When you've got thousands of independent fishermen, to control them and regulate them, it's hard. So, it appears that that's what they want to do, is get the independent little guy out of it. And just have to deal with a bunch of big guys. Which I think would be a shame. They've been crying about the demise of the family farm for 50 years. It still continues, but I think, hopefully, it won't happen. It certainly won't happen in my lifetime, and hopefully won't happen in my kid's lifetime.

The guys that don't have a lot of debt are going to be able to hang on, and I see a light at the end of the tunnel. I don't think that you'll ever see fishing as a way to get rich quick, or anything like that. But, I think it will continue to be a viable activity. I hope to see it improve. I think we're at a particularly low ebb right now, because of a lot of things. As I say, too many big boats built that aren't owner-operated, which–the fact that their stocks are depleted and you can't make any money–that's going to get the investors out of it. That's going to help. And hopefully, most of the guys that are fishing that want to stay fishing will be able to hang on.

Dick Bardwell

I think with the proper management of the fishermen, we will survive. It's going to be tough. I think what's going to happen is when the federal government gets their hand in your pocket too deep, people are going to revolt, like we revolted on the fluke last winter. We're going to take steps to have things corrected. I'm not a law-breaker. If the law says I can't do it, I won't do it. But what I will do is take steps to have the law changed so it benefits the majority. This I will do. But I won't break the law intentionally. I think with the proper management of the fishermen themselves and their own business and a little leniency on this other stuff–get us back the northeast peak [of Georges Bank], put the Hague Line [dividing the U.S. and Canadian waters on Georges Bank] where it belongs, keep the politics out of it. And I think things will be just fine.

Walter Allyn

"

Emptying a lobster pot.

"The weak will drop, they're going to drop. Just like any other business. If there's fourteen grocery stores in a row, there's only going to be two or three survive. If the guy's capable, he'll survive. If he maintains his equipment, keeps his good show on the road, he'll survive. It'll be tough, but he'll do it.

People are talking now about the government subsidizing us. I don't want welfare. I don't want that. I want the right to work. That's what I want. I want a fair price for my product. Stop some of these imports. If the politicians want to do something in a political way to help the American people, buy American. Stop imports on fishery products, on food products or whatever. We don't need theirs, they need ours.

Walter Allyn

I don't see any future in the business with the government interfering now.

Jim Allyn

I'd like to say that you're your own boss. You could say that four years ago. But now you can't fish on what you want to fish on. You can't do this, you can't do that. So really you're not your own boss anymore. You're dictated by the laws, as to what you can fish, when you can fish. It used to be relaxing. You'd go out, you'd make your living, you'd come in. Now, you've got the financial burden of the laws. It's not very much fun anymore. It used to be fun. Used to look forward to coming down in the morning, have coffee, leave, joke, laugh, never think twice. You know you're gonna make a check. It's changed, really has. Last two years. Last two years, it's really gotten worse. I don't see it gettin' any better. It's a dying occupation.

Al Maderia

If a fisherman can make a living, he will. If he can't, he'll get out of it.

Robert Berg

Ten years ago there was a lot of fish and now there's not too many fish, but who's to say in ten years from now there could be more fish again. And you know, it could be a whole different ball game. But right now, it's pretty scarce. Between all the regulations and the lack of fish, and the price of gear, and the price of everything, it's pretty much a scary business to be in. It's hard.

Phil Torres

Right now, everything's up in the air. Fishermen don't have any idea where the industry's going. I look at John Rita, who has three kids. And John doesn't know if he's going to be fishing a year from today. I know John will be the last fisherman to go out if small fishermen die out. He sees it might happen, but fishermen, because they're so independent, they will fight things, and they will work as hard as they can. And I think right now the money aspect is very, very difficult."

Michael Medeiros

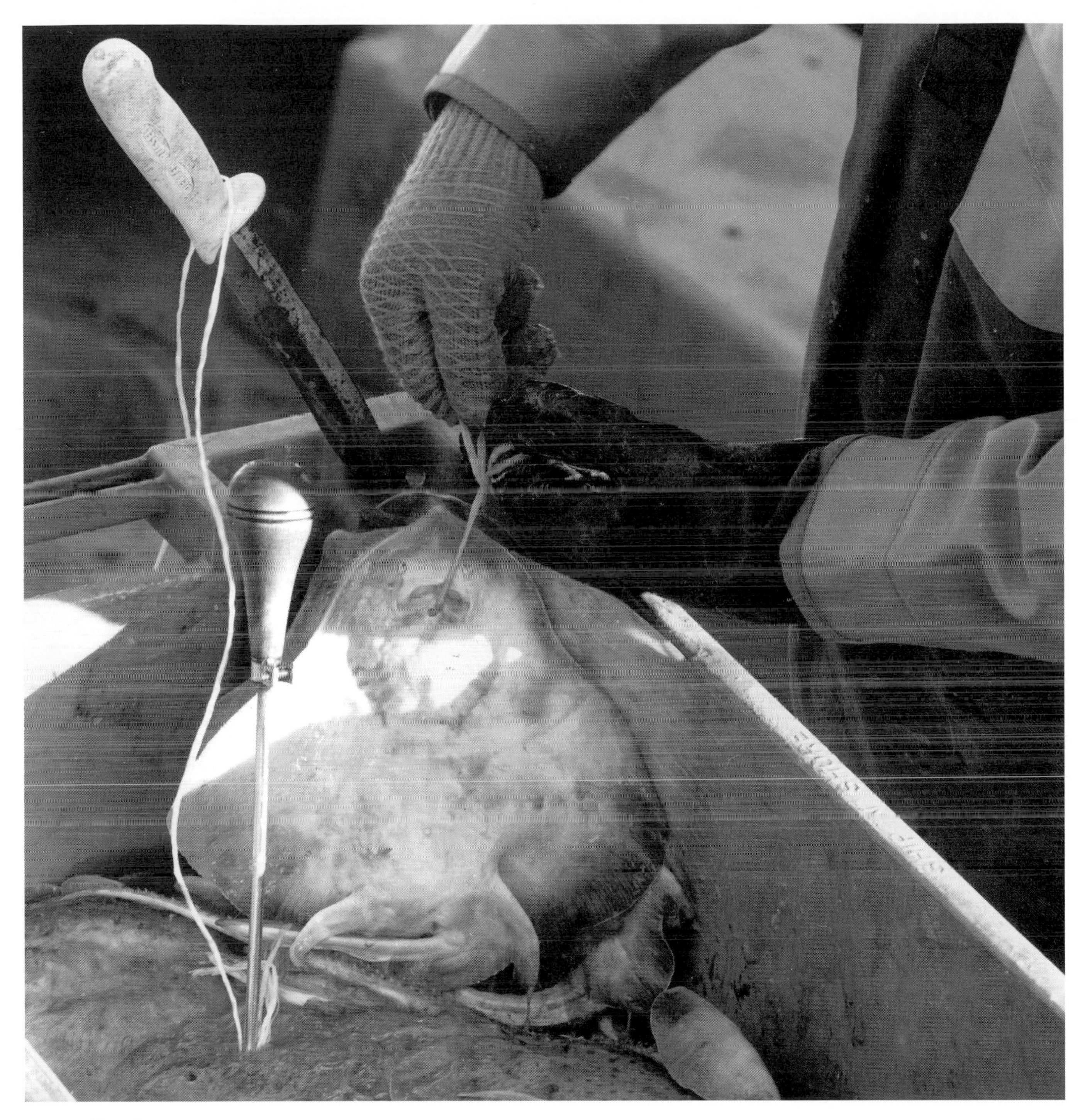

Stringing lobster bait.

"

That's just too many big boats. Too many boats. Too many big boats, that aren't even paid for. They can't even pay the interest on these boats. This has been going on for years and years but the boats keep working.

You know, I been over 40, 40-some years in this business. I want to retire. I can't retire because the government has got the fishing in such a predicament that you can't even sell a boat. Who the hell wants, no one in their right mind would go into this business. You know? There's no future. There could be a future because, believe me, they don't need to regulate twine size or anything else. All they've got to is get rid of the pressure. And the fish will make it. They get rid of the horsepower, and get rid of the boats, be right back where we were. Fish would be fine.

Charlie Fellows

And unfortunately, the reproductive patterns of the fish don't keep up with the increases in technology. So, I think it's a time of reckoning for fishermen, and to really find out what is best for the industry. And no one wants to see themselves or a friend go out of business, but that's where things are headed.

Michael Medeiros

You could take my two boys, for example. They're individuals, they're proud individuals. And they take great pride in what they do. And they also take great pride in their vessels. It's a heritage. It's a way of life. Good or bad. And we'll be there, we're not going anywhere. In spite of everybody.

Walter Allyn

There's times it's good money and there's times it's not. It has been better. I would have put that on the top of the list, eight or ten years ago, the money's good. Today, it is not the money that keeps us here.

And whatever happens here in the next five, is going to really tell the story. So come back in five years. If I'm still here, I'll give you another story.

Tim Medeiros

This is their livelihood. I don't think that they're going to deplete it by overfishing it. Because they know themselves, once they overfish it, once the fish are gone, they're finished. So they're not about to do that.

If it dies, the fishermen are going to be the ones who are hurt. They know it. I don't think they're going to let that happen to themselves. Not because there's rules and regulations that prohibit them from doing if, but because they don't want to see it end. Like I said, my husband loves fishing and he wouldn't want to see it end. I think he'll go on until he can't fish any longer.

Ann Rita

"

Conclusion

Dockside Reflections, March 2004

As a brisk wind drives a few frozen snowflakes through the clear air, wire rigging slaps metal masts, twanging harshly. A handful of work trucks and cars populate the large but almost vacant parking lot that abuts the Stonington Fishermen's Dock. No signs warn off trespassers. They are not needed. The stacks of lobster pots, hulking scallop dredges, and plastic bait barrels mark the boundaries of a working waterfront untouched by the surrounding gentrification.

The dock has a particular smell, an amalgam of bait, lines encrusted with drying sea vegetation, old paint, creosoted timbers, and salt water. This is a charming smell for fishermen. Slightly sweet and a little pungent, it can be found at cold-water fishing docks the world over. It is not found anywhere else.

Most of the current fleet is in. A quick count reveals between 25 and 30 boats. They range in size and sophistication from a simple open-decked outboard-motor-powered boat up to a powerful red vessel nearing 100 feet in length: the largest and most modern looking of a substantial scallop dredging fleet. Perhaps 10 of these powerful steel boats lie quietly in port on this late winter day. On the smaller pier next to some lobster boats, three men are engaged in conversation.

Scant blocks away, two of Stonington's Water Street restaurants are doing a slow but modest business catering to a well-heeled "local" trade. The human contrast between the docks and the restaurants is not as extreme as one might predict. The men in both places appear to be over 50, with some substantially older. Both groups have the freedom to stop and visit during a time of the day when most others are at work.

The obvious similarities end there. The men in the restaurant wear mostly casual but expensive clothing. Their cheeks radiate a comfortable pink glow. Unchallenged hands, well manicured and rather small, raise glasses of club soda and chardonnay. The faces on the dock, by contrast, have an abraded red look—part today's wind, part a lifetime of exposure to the weather with little time for moisturizers. The fishermen's hands appear swollen, each packed with enough meat to make a good fillet.

The coexistence of these groups of men and the worlds of Water Street and the Town Dock may represent one of the most distinguishing features in the contemporary history of commercial fishing out of Stonington. Although high property values have led or forced Stonington's historical fishing families to relocate outside of the Borough, the industry has retained a dedicated space on the village waterfront. The Town Dock provides the central place that commercial fishing in Stonington needs to survive, not just as an economic activity, but also as a community. No other town in Connecticut has taken such deliberate steps to support its commercial fishing industry. No other town in Connecticut has an identifiable cohesive fishing community.

Troubling times faced Stonington fishermen when the oral histories on which this book are based were collected by Mystic Seaport in 1993 through 1996. Restrictions on fishing time, larger mesh sizes, and strict quotas for specific species were becoming a significant hardship to a New

England fishing industry used to management by market forces, natural cycles, and weather. But fishermen have always faced doubtful futures, and longtime fishing families are the masters of managing uncertainty. Saving during flush times, targeting a different species of fish, buying or selling boats, taking a temporary or part-time job on shore—the flexibility imparted by these other strategies has allowed some fishermen from Stonington and other coastal communities to survive difficult periods.

Despite complaints of falling revenues, and predictions of impending doom, fishing out of Stonington has survived a full decade since the interviews took place. In some respects, the area around the Town Dock in March 2004 presents evidence of this continued vitality and economic success. There are no abandoned or nearly abandoned boats; no obvious evidence of makeshift maintenance; no fishing boats in federal custody for nonpayment of bills. A closer look at the most rusty looking trawler reveals a stack of empty paint cans and the smooth gloss of gray primer inside the bulwarks. Even the *Neptune*, an anachronistic looking eastern-rig dragger, presents some signs of prosperity, or at least hope. A well-tended trawl hangs suspended from the rigging. Shiny new cables glimmer from the drums of her well-used trawl winch. The perimeter of the dock provides more evidence: nets carefully stacked and sheltered from the weather; freezer boxes and working fish trucks. Very telling are large piles of discarded or, more accurately, permanently stored fishing gear (fishermen by nature and experience rarely throw anything away). A pair of decaying wooden otter trawl doors rest easily in the weeds. Ten yards away a slightly larger door, this one made from steel, exhibits signs of a bad day at sea. Wrenched out of shape from contact with a rocky hang or a wreck, the door speaks of critical fishing time lost and thousands of dollars spent to repair and replace gear. Another door shows evidence of alteration: weight added to increase efficiency—possibly to allow the towing of a larger net. Nearby, an old scallop dredge awaits reactivation. Scallop dredges, like fishermen, weather slowly.

Despite outward signs of durability, the future of commercial fishing at Stonington remains uncertain. Economics, culture, and time are weakening the bonds that have held the local fishing community together for generations. The active fishing community is aging. In a 1998 survey of New England fishing communities, the youngest fisherman reported in Stonington was 32.[1] The children of the present generation are choosing other lines of work. A partial explanation for this may be the presence of more plentiful and diverse job opportunities on shore. Some fishermen believe that the younger generation simply do not like the difficulty and danger of fishing. This may be true, but some fishermen's sons have always chosen a working life on shore.

The breaking of work-centered intergenerational ties also reflects the changing economics of commercial fishing out of Stonington. Youngsters of 11 or 12 can be a real asset in a small-scale fishing operation. Their duties expand as they grow in body and in knowledge—knowledge that they gain by working with older family members, often their fathers or uncles. Such organic relationships provide for a seamless (although not necessarily trouble-free) transition between generations. However, highly capitalized 80-foot draggers working within tightly scheduled and intensely regulated fisheries offer little place for the very young. The gear is too big and dangerous and the economic stakes too high. In such an industrial place, the old family work bonds have little space to form.

If unnourished by common working experiences, existing links to family working and ethnic traditions will not last forever. Because fishing families no longer share common neighborhoods within the Borough, it is less likely that children will take an active interest in the business. Living in diverse neighborhoods, playing and going to school with children from a wide variety of socio-economic and ethnic backgrounds, the children and grandchildren of fishermen today are more apt to identify with the cultural mainstream. As a continuing tradition, the annual blessing of the fleet is a reminder that a commercial fishing community still exists in Stonington. It suggests this community may continue to survive for generations to come.

In 1976, Congress passed the most powerful fisheries law in United States history. The Magnuson Fishery Conservation and Management Act (now called the Magnuson-Stevens Act) declared that all fisheries within 200 miles of the coast belonged to the United States. Before the act, large, highly capitalized foreign fleets dominated the richest fishing grounds on the North American continental shelf. By claiming these resources (as other nations had done with their offshore waters), the act also initiated a revitalization of America's aged and inefficient fishing industry. Tax incentives and low-interest/high-risk credit programs targeted toward the fishing industry promoted a phenomenal increase in the numbers and efficiency of the nation's commercial fishing vessels. Ironically, in the 1950s, fishing industry analysts worried about the under-production of fish by the U.S. fleet. By the 1980s, it was clear that overproduction represented the real danger.

The Magnuson Act also established the framework for what has become, in the minds of fishermen and environmental activists alike, a regulatory nightmare. States control the natural resources that fall within 3 miles of their coasts. The 197 miles of Exclusive Economic Zone (EEZ) created by the Magnuson Act, however, fall under federal jurisdiction. For Stonington fishermen, the principal regulating body for this is the New England Fisheries Management Council. The council includes state and federal environmental regulators as well as commercial and recreational fishermen, fishing industry representatives, and environmental advocates. It is not a happy mix. The National Marine Fisheries Service provides the science needed to manage the fisheries, but the council—at least until recent years—set the regulations. Commercial fishing interests, in general, dominated the New England Council during its first two decades of operation. Fish regulations, while significant, did not adequately protect many fish species.[2]

Serious change began in 1996, Congress passed the Sustainable Fisheries Act, which reauthorized, renamed, and amended the Magnuson Act. The new Magnuson-Stevens Fishery Conservation and Management Act recognized that increased fishing pressure, weak management schemes, and habitat destruction threatened to damage irreversibly the fisheries resources of the United States.[3] For Stonington fishermen, new regulation has brought both gains and losses.

Life continues to change for Stonington fishermen. Old fishermen living today came of age during a tumultuous period in world history. Expanding world populations, international conflicts, technological change, and economic globalization are just a few covering labels for planet-altering processes that have had a direct effect on the lives of fishermen. Fifty years ago, when men such as Art Medeiros were young fishermen, the annual world commercial fishing harvest was perhaps 40 billion pounds. Since that time, the world commercial harvest has gone up by at least 500 or 600 percent. Southern New England's overall harvest has not changed that much, but the size of the largest boats and the range of species harvested through the region has changed radically. The development of the 200-mile limit gave U.S. fishermen uncontested access to offshore continental shelf fisheries. The presence of large western-rig steel draggers is one effect of the expanded fishing grounds.

Expanded commercial fishing efforts, competition for resources with recreational sports fishermen, and the development of aggressive and articulate environmental organizations are among the major factors that led to the imposition of stronger commercial fishing regulations. It is hard to overestimate the economic and psychological effects these regulations have had on New England fishermen during the past decade. Identifying and measuring these effects, however, is both difficult and controversial. Causes and effects are difficult to prove. Current shifts in the fortunes of fishermen exclusively attributed to regulations may have other deeper causes and direct historical parallels. For example, the number of boats fishing out of Stonington has fluctuated, sometimes dramatically, over the past 50 years—long before modern fisheries regulations came to the region.

Statistics suggest that Stonington fishermen did pretty well during the second half of the 1990s. In 1999, 75 commercial fishing licenses listed Stonington as the home port. Among this group were 36 lobster, 20 rod-and-reel, 15 trawling, and 3 gillnet licenses. Despite frequent negative press, landings of groundfish in Connecticut (the vast majority of which come from Stonington vessels) fluctuated but showed a substantial overall increase. In 1996, vessels home ported in Connecticut landed 169,000 pounds of groundfish. In 2000, this figure reached 3,227,000 pounds. Scallop fishermen have also done very well. Landings by Connecticut boats in 1996 amounted to 400,404 pounds of the succulent white disks. The harvest for 2002 reached 1,578,640 pounds. Stock assessments publicized in the spring of 2004 put the biomass of harvestable scallops at record levels—a fact reflected in the volume of large low-priced scallops available in regional grocery stores.[4]

Lobster fishing, a mainstay of small- to medium-size boats up and down the Connecticut coast, had some banner years. In 1994, 2,200,000 pounds of the tasty crustaceans were delivered in the state. By 1998, the figure had risen to 3,700,000 pounds. The lobster bubble burst with little warning in 1999. A massive die-off of lobsters in western Long Island Sound sent alarm throughout Connecticut ports. While this initially had little effect on Stonington lobstermen, whose grounds lay outside of the impact area, the die-off signaled the beginning of a serious reversal for lobstermen statewide. Research continues on the cause of the die-off, but many believe that it reflects a combination of factors. Recent studies have shown that Malathion, a pesticide used to combat the mosquito-born West Nile virus in 1999, is particularly toxic to the lobster. Heavy rainfall runoff carried the pesticide into the Sound in higher than expected concentrations. Low dissolved oxygen levels brought about by higher water temperatures may have reduced the resistance of lobsters. Experts also identified overfishing as part of the matrix.[5]

Unfortunately, the downturn in lobstering is not confined to western Long Island Sound. A parasitic shell disease that may affect fertility has been spreading northward for the past several years. Lobster landings in Connecticut barely passed 1,000,000 pounds in 2002 and will continues to drop in the near future as new regulations increasing the minimum harvestable size go into effect. Other Southern New England states are also suffering declines.[6]

The scallop fishery shows that regulations can have positive environmental effects. Most fishermen today recognize that regulations are necessary. Many fishermen believe, and some reputable scientific studies have confirmed, that many fish stocks have recovered measurably, partly due to protection from harvesting, partly due to natural cycles. Overall, however, Stonington fishermen, like those in many New England ports, appear to be losing more ground than they have gained. Regulatory regimes are increasingly restrictive. Fishermen consider them unfair and often just stupid.

Species-specific quotas cause tremendous frustration for Stonington draggers. These quotas have cut their livelihood by reducing harvest levels and by disturbing traditional marketing patterns. The fishermen have faced an odd economic dilemma. In some cases, they are harvesting fewer fish of a particular species and receiving a lower price. Quotas lead to large concentrations of fish flooding the market and forcing down prices. Quotas and by-catch regulations play havoc with inshore fishermen. For the past several years, regulations have fishermen such as Al Maderia Jr., owner of the well-kept 55-foot wooden dragger *Serena* to dump hundreds of pounds of dead but perfectly edible fluke (summer flounder) and other fish back into ocean. "The laws" he explained to a local reporter, "take an honest fisherman and turn him into a crook." "Who eats them? The seagulls!" another disgusted captain complained in an earlier report.[7]

Recent court actions have made things far worse. A Conservation Law Foundation lawsuit filed in 2000 charged that the National Marine Fisheries Service and the New England Fisheries Management Council were not adequately protecting groundfish stocks from overfishing. A series of federal court decisions by Judge Gladys Kessler ruled in their favor and paved the way for sweeping new restrictions. In 2002, temporary regulations reduced the allowed number of days at sea for trawlers from an annual maximum of 88 down to 70. More deep cutbacks are on the horizon. The effects of regulation do not fall evenly. Many boats receive far less than the maximum time. Again, small operators restricted to local waters are hurt the most. Some public officials are now predicting the end of inshore fishing out of Stonington.[8]

The current bogeyman, Amendment 13 of the New England Ground Fish Management Plan, reflects a court-directed mandate to create a significant reduction in fish mortality by restricting commercial fishing. Eliminating days at sea and reducing the number of vessels operating in New England will, regulators and environmental advocates insist, stop current practices they consider "overfishing." The goal is to reach a complete "recovery" of all stocks by 2009.

The irony for fishermen is that they have learned to work within what they already consider a restrictive regulatory system. By shifting to other stocks, altering their gear, and providing detailed catch information to state and federal regulators, fishermen believe that they have already sacrificed much. And, in their collective opinion, the larger numbers of fish that they are seeing in their nets offer proof that they have done enough. Amendment 13 of the Northeast Multispecies Fishery Management Plan privileges the rapid recovery of all fish stocks above the maintenance of viable commercial infrastructure and the maintenance of traditional fishing communities. The Final Environmental Impact Statement and Regulatory Flexibility Analysis for Amendment 13 argue that its policies "are intended to ensure that a sustainable fishery is attained in the long term." The Statement also offers this chilling forecast:

Some of the effects on fishing communities may be irreversible, such as losses in shoreside infrastructure and gentrification of the waterfront in response to reductions in the fishing fleet. As a result, the benefits that will ultimately accrue from the rebuilding program may not be realized by current participants in the fishery. . . . In general, measures which reduce fishing effort will have a negative cumulative effect on fishery participants while producing a positive effect on the resource and the habitat.[9]

Responses to tighter regulations that took effect in 2002 underscore the stressed condition of Stonington's commercial fishing industry. A *New York Times* article from August 2002 ran the headline "An Old Fleet Under a Dark Cloud." The sympathetic article describes the effects of recent reduction in landings. The town's remaining major wholesale fish buyer reported major consolidations and cutbacks. Wilcox Marine Supply, a family-run firm that specializes in commercial fishing gear, sold its building in Mystic and reduced its staff from eleven to just two people. Wilcox has operated in the area for over 120 years; the question remains—how much longer can they last. Also reflecting economic problems and deeper community changes, Joe Rendeiro retired from fishing after 51 years. He was finding it harder and harder to recruit skilled crewmen.[10] Commercial fishing groups and marine social scientists have been warning for years about infrastructure erosion in fishing communities. Web pages and newsletters from environmental and recreational fishing groups do not sound the trumpet about these losses.

Hard times are easy for fishermen to dwell on. They also attract much attention from outsiders who seek to understand fishermen's lives. In some respects all times are hard. Bad weather never goes out of fashion. Fishermen find too few fish, or too many fish and low prices. They may return to find no market, or a dishonest market. The regulations just keep coming. Good or bad, fair or unfair, they all make life harder. Then there are engines to overhaul, boats to rebuild, gear to mend, and gear to buy. The present, even when the money is good, is just the present. It offers a welcome break from more nagging worries and a time to buy something extra for the home or the boat—a time to set something aside for the harder days ahead.

The deeper meanings of commercial fishing as an individual calling and as a community culture find their best expression in personal reflections and shared stories, in the connections between men and women of all generations whose lives this unique industry has shaped. The interviews included in this book capture more than moments in time in the mid-1990s. They record the memories, values, and collective heart of an intact fishing community with a long history—one that has successfully navigated through decades of change and challenges. Despite the dark forecasts on the fishing horizon, a vital fleet fishes out of Stonington in 2004. History suggests that it will be there, in some form, in 2014. Real fishermen are tough. Stonington fishermen are real.

Joe Rendeiro's words to high-ranking officials during a 2002 meeting at the Town Dock say enough.

"I quit fishing, but I didn't quit fighting. And I won't quit fighting until they shovel dirt on my face."[11]

JOHN O. JENSEN

Notes

Notes to Introduction, pages 15-35

1. Warren Boeschenstein, *Historic American Towns along the Atlantic Coast* (Baltimore and London: The Johns Hopkins University Press, 1999), 119; Stonington, Connecticut, *Town Report*, 1965.

2. Stonington, *Town Report, 1965.*

3. Jerome S. Anderson, *Anderson's Stonington Directory, 1881, Containing A General Directory of the Citizens and a Complete Business Directory and Register of Stonington Borough and the Villages of Mystic, Mystic Bridge, and Pawcatuck* (Stonington: Jerome Anderson, 1881), 20; Richard A. Wheeler, *History of the Town of Stonington* (New London: Press of the Day Publishing Company,1900), 33; John C. Pearson, ed., *The Fish and Fisheries of Colonial North America, part 2, The New England States* (Washington, D.C.: National Marine Fisheries Service, 1972), 268, in Kevin Dwyer, "The *Emma C. Berry,*" Research Report, Documentation Office, Henry B. du Pont Preservation Shipyard, Mystic Seaport, Mystic, Connecticut.

4. Log of sloop *Resolution*, 1803-04, OLog 5, G.W. Blunt White Library, Mystic Seaport; Jefferson B. Browne, *Key West: The Old and the New* (St. Augustine, Florida: Record Company, 1912), 7-8, quoted in Dwyer, "The *Emma C. Berry*"; Howard I. Chapelle, *The National Watercraft Collection*, 2nd ed. (Washington, D.C.: Smithsonian Institution, 1976), 221-22; see also William N. Peterson, *Mystic Built: Ships and Shipyards of the Mystic River, Connecticut, 1784-1919* (Mystic: Mystic Seaport, 1989); Dwyer, "The *Emma C. Berry.*"

5. John C. Pease and John M. Niles, *A Gazeteer of Connecticut and Rhode Island* (Hartford: William S. March, 1819), 141, in Dwyer, "The *Emma C. Berry*"; Priscilla Jennings Slanetz, "A History of the Fulton Fish Market," *The Log of Mystic Seaport* 38:2 (Spring 1986): 21; Katherine B. Crandall, *The Fine Old Town of Stonington* (Westerly, Rhode Island: Utter Company, 1949), 127-28; John H. Matthews, "A History of the Fishing Industry of New York," *Fishing Gazette Annual Review* (1929): 52, in Dwyer, "The *Emma C. Berry*"; "Profiles: Dragger Captain," *The New Yorker,* January 8, 1947, 32.

6. Much has been written about Stonington's whalers and sealers, see most particularly Richard M. Jones, "Stonington Borough: A Connecticut Seaport in the Nineteenth Century" (PhD diss., City University of New York, 1976); see too, Henry R. Palmer, *Stonington By the Sea* (Stonington: Palmer Press, 1957); John Hayward, *The New England Gazetteer* (Boston: John Hayward; Concord, New Hampshire: Boyd and White, 1839).

7. Albert Van Dusen, *Connecticut* (New York: Random House, 1961), 321-23; William Haynes, *1649-1949 Stonington Chronology* (Stonington: Pequot Press, 1949), 62, 94.

8. George Brown Goode, ed., *The Fisheries and Fishery Industries of the U.S., 7* vols., (Washington, D.C.: Government Printing Office, 1884-87), sect. 5, 315, 711; James L. Wallace, "Fishery Harbor Development: A Case Study of a Connecticut Coastal Community, Stonington, Connecticut" (master's thesis, University of Rhode Island, 1984), ch. 2, 2; *Anderson's Stonington Directory, 1881*, 62.

9. Wallace, "Fishery Harbor Development," ch. 2, 2; Ellery Thompson, *Draggerman's Haul* (New York: Viking Press, 1950), 179.

10. Andrew W. German, "Otter Trawling Comes to America: The Bay State Fishing Company, 1905-1938," *The American Neptune* 44:2 (Spring 1984): 114-15; Frank H. Wood, "Trawling and Dragging in New England Waters," *The Atlantic Fisherman*, February 1926, 11.

11. Wood, "Trawling and Dragging in New England Waters," January, February 1926; Donald Lewis, "Stonington's Portuguese Fishermen," *Historical Footnotes, Bulleting of the Stonington Historical Society,* August 1965, 7; Jacob Hotsky, interview by Elena Martin, November 5, 1986, OH 86-5, G.W. Blunt White Library, Mystic Seaport.

12. Thompson, *Draggerman's Haul*, 32.

13. Manuel Maderia, interview by Glenn Gordinier, July 26, 1993, OH 93-19, G.W. Blunt White Library; Henry R. Palmer Jr., "Boatbuilding in Stonington," *The Log of Mystic Seaport* 28:3 (October 1976): 87-88.

14. Lewis, "Stonington's Portuguese Fishermen," 8.

15. Thompson, *Draggerman's Haul*, 57; George A. Berg, interview by Fred Calabretta and Glenn Gordinier, June 8, 1993, OH 93-13, G.W. Blunt White Library; Lewis, "Stonington's Portuguese Fishermen," 8.

16. Crandall, *Fine Old Town of Stonington*, 131; *Stonington Industries* (Stonington: Industrial Committee of the Stonington Tricentennial, 1949), 14, 18; Thompson, *Draggerman's Haul*, 194; Walter Ansel, "The Dragger *Florence*," *The Log of Mystic Seaport* 36:4 (Winter 1985): 119-21.

17. Benjamin A.G. Fuller, "Coming of the Explosive Engine," *The Log of Mystic Seaport* 45:2 (Autumn 1993): 34; Lewis, "Stonington's Portuguese Fishermen," 7; Crandall, *Fine Old Town of Stonington*, 131.

18. Wood, "Trawling and Dragging in New England Waters," February 1926, 24; Lewis, "Stonington's Portuguese Fishermen," 6, 8; Thompson, *Draggerman's Haul*, 68, 168.

19. Howard F. Burdick, *The Southern New England Fishermen's Association, Inc., Year Book, 1935* (Mystic: Riverside Press, 1935), 5, 6-7, 9-11; Howard F. Burdick, ed., *The Southern New England Fisherman's Association Year Book, 1936* (Mystic: Riverside Press, 1936), title page, 17, 19; *National Fisherman*, April 1959, 24; as one member of the brotherhood put it, "due to the effect of federal law, state law, county laws, by-laws, corporation laws, brother-in-laws, mother-in-laws, and outlaws," fishermen had been "held down, held up, walked on, sat on, flattened and squeezed," Burdick, *Year Book, 1936*, 31.

20. Burdick, *Year Book, 1936*, 17; see also Carl Gersuny, John J. Poggie Jr., Robert J. Marshall, *Some Effects of Technological Change on New England Fishermen* (Kingston: University of Rhode Island, 1975), 17-23.

21. Burdick, *Year Book, 1936*, 7; James Henry, interview by Glenn Gordinier, September 22, 1993, OH 93-14, G.W. Blunt White Library.

22. Thompson, *Draggerman's Haul*, 229-31; Everett Allen, *A Wind to Shake the World* (Boston: Little, Brown, 1976), 142; Berg, interview; Palmer, "Boatbuilding in Stonington," 86.

23. Wallace, "Fishery Harbor Development," ch. 2, 2; Palmer, "Boatbuilding in Stonington," 86.

24. Wallace, "Fishery Harbor Development," ch. 2, 2; "Profiles: Dragger Captain," 32.

25. Blanche Stillman, interview by Fred Calabretta, 1993, OH 93-59, G.W. Blunt White Library; *National Fisherman*, April 1959, 24; Anthony Bailey, *In the Village* (New York: Alfred A. Knopf, 1971), 133.

26. Thomas R. Lewis and John E. Harmon, *Connecticut: A Geography* (Boulder and London: Westview Press, 1986), 193; "Profiles: Dragger Captain," 32.

27. Ansel, "Dragger *Florence*," 118-25; "Profiles: Dragger Captain," 32; Palmer, "Boatbuilding in Stonington," 87, 88; Wallace, "Fishery Harbor Development," ch. 2, 1.

28. James Allyn, interview by Glenn Gordinier, October 29, 1993, OH 93-44, G.W. Blunt White Library; Bernard L. Gordon, "Ellery Franklin Thompson: Fisherman, Author, and Marine Painter," *The Log of Mystic Seaport* 41:3-4 (Fall 1989/Winter 1990): 100-104; Joseph Mitchell, *At the Bottom of the Harbor* (Boston: Little, Brown, 1959); "Connecticut Fleet Gets 62-Foot *Our Gang*," *Atlantic Fisherman*, August 1946, 3; "Connecticut Fleet Has Several Additions," *Atlantic Fisherman*, September 1946, 40; "Profiles: Dragger Captain," 32.

29. Thompson, *Draggerman's Haul*, 173; Wallace, "Fishery Harbor Development," ch. 3, 2; "Profiles: Dragger Captain," 32; Jacob Hotsky, interview; Vivian Volovar, interview by Fred Calabretta, October 27, 1993, OH 93-47, G.W. Blunt White Library; Ellery Thompson, *Come Aboard the Draggers* (Stonington: Stonington Publishers, 1958), 52, 56.

30. *Atlantic Fisherman*, February 1950, 24; October 1950, 31; November 1950, 26-27.

31. "Fish Landings For the Month of May," *Atlantic Fisherman*, June 1950, 40; "Fish Landings For the Month January," *Atlantic Fisherman*, February 1951, 35.

32. "The Southern New England Fisheries," *National Fisherman*, April 1959, 23-24; Thompson, *Come Aboard the Draggers*, 54.

33. Wallace, "Fishery Harbor Development," ch. ?, 31; Gersuny, Poggie et al., *Some Effects of Technological Change*, 25; David Boeri and James Gibson, *"Tell it Good-Bye, Kiddo": The Decline of the New England Offshore Fishery* (Camden, Maine: International Marine Publishing, 1976), 117-23; Arthur Medeiros, interview by Fred Calabretta, May 18, 1993, OH 93-18, G.W. Blunt White Library.

34. Peter V. Fossel, "The Past Is Present in Stonington," *Gloucester: The Magazine of the New England Coast*, 3:1, 39.

35. Fossel, "Past Is Present in Stonington," 38; Wallace, "Fishery Harbor Development," ch. 2, 2; Bailey, *In the Village*, 133-36; Manuel Maderia, interview; "Connecticut's Proposed Trash Fish Plant Meets Opposition," *National Fisherman*, December 1954, 43; "Bill Would Ban Trash Plants," *National Fisherman*, March 1955, 51; "Bill Banning Trash Fish Plant Killed," *National Fisherman*, July 1955, 43; Wallace, "Fishery Harbor Development," ch. 2, 2-3.

36. Wallace, "Fishery Harbor Development," ch. 2, 2-3; "Properties Ownership," *National Register of Historic Places Inventory: Nomination Form*, 1979, 1-15.

37. Grand List, Town of Stonington; Boeschenstein, *Historic American Towns*, 132; Fossel, "Past Is Present in Stonington," 39; "Description," *National Register of Historic Places Inventory: Nomination Form*, 1979, 3.

38. Lewis, "Stonington's Portuguese Fishermen," 1, 6.

39. Mary Maderia and Manuel Maderia, "Captain St. Peter," *Historical Footnotes, Bulletin of the Stonington Historical Society*, August 1973; Manuel Maderia, interview.

40. Bailey, *In the Village*, 130-31; Thompson, *Draggerman's Haul*, 181; Elizabeth Fellows, interview by Glenn Gordinier, December 12, 1993, OH 93-54, G.W. Blunt White Library; Ann M. Rita, interview by Glenn Gordinier, October 4, 1993, OH 93-37, G.W. Blunt White Library; Frank Keane, interview by Glenn Gordinier, July 28, 1994, OH 94-31, G.W. Blunt White Library.

41. Arthur Medeiros, interview; Walter Allyn, interview by Glenn Gordinier, June 25, 1993, OH 93-6, G.W. Blunt White Library.

42. James Henry, interview; Manuel Maderia, interview; Blanche Stillman, interview.

43. "Stonington Has Real 'Fishing Family,'" *Atlantic Fisherman*, April 1950, 33; Thompson, *Draggerman's Haul*, 250-53; Bailey, *In the Village*, 132.

44. Mary Maderia and Manuel Maderia, "Captain St. Peter."

45. Elizabeth Fellows, interview.

46. Manuel Maderia, interview; James Henry, interview; Arthur Medeiros, interview; Blanche Stillman, interview; Al and Patty Banks, interview by Fred Calabretta, July 2, 1993, OH 93-8, G.W. Blunt White Library.

47. Palmer, "Boatbuilding in Stonington," 83; Gersuny, Poggie, et al., *Some Effects of Technological Change*, 17.

48. U.S. Bureau of the Census, Census, Town of Stonington, 1980, 1990. The 1980 population count for the Borough was very near the count of 1,200 reported in 1839, when whaling and steamboating dominated the community; George A. Berg, interview; Walter Allyn, interview; James Henry, interview; Manuel Maderia, interview.

49. Ann Rita, interview; Richard Bardwell, interview by Glenn Gordinier, December 9, 1993, OH 93-57, G.W. Blunt White Library; Wallace, "Fishery Harbor Development," ch. 2, 2.

50. Wallace, "Fishery Harbor Development," ch. 2, 2; Frank Keane, interview.

51. Wallace, "Fishery Harbor Development," ch. 1, 5, ch. 3, 1; James Henry, interview; Lewis and Harmon, *Connecticut: A Geography*, 193.

Notes to Conclusion, pages 212-217

1. Madeline Hall-Arber, et, al. *New England's Fishing Communities*, (MIT Sea Grant) (http://web.mit.edu/afs/athena/org/s/sea grant/advisory/marfin), 64.

2. New England Fisheries Management Council Web site Home Page. http://www.nefmc.org/about/index.html; William McClosky, *Their Fathers' Work: Casting Nets with the World's Fishermen* rev.ed. (Camden, Maine: International Marine/ Rugged Mountain Press, 2000), 338-39.

3. Magnuson-Stevens Fishery Conservation and Management Act Public Law 94-265. http://www.nmfs.noaa.gov/sfa/magact/mag1.html#s2

4. Arber, *New England's Fishing Communities*, 56; Northeast Multispecies Amendment 13 SEIS, December 18, 2003. vol. 2, 1370. http://www.nefmc.org/nemulti/index.html; National Marine Fisheries Service Landings Database. Query Results, Connecticut Sea Scallops (www.st.nmfs.gov/pls/webpls/MF_ANNUAL_LANDINGS .RESULTSNMFS); *National Fisherman*, April 2004, 30.

5. *Boston Globe*, March 7, 2003.

6. National Marine Fisheries Service Landings Database. Query Results, lobster; *Boston Globe*, March 7, 2003.

7. *Westerly Sun*, 2 September 2003, November 17, 2000.

8. Conservation Law Foundation Advocacy New and Updates, May 22, 2000 (http://www.clf.org/hot/20000523.htm); *New York Times*, Connecticut Weekly Desk, August 18, 2002.

9. Northeast Multi Species Amendment 13 SEIS, December 18, 2003, vol. 1, xiv.

10. *New York Times*, Connecticut Weekly Desk, August 18, 2002.

11. *Westerly Sun*, August 31, 2002.

"In Memory of Fishermen Who Died at Sea"

Arthur Arruda
Albert Maderia
Arthur Maderia
Roderick DeBragga and Son
Rodney DeBragga
Joey Roderick
Charlie Brennen
Kenneth R. Gould
Raymond V. Morris III
Manual Fayal Rezendes
William Joseph Litke
Dean C. Harvey
Norman Riley
Scott Russell
Ellis Moffitt
Bob Moran
George Roderick
Douglas Warner
Roger Noel
John Houser
Michael N. Hare
Robert A. Cale
Herbert L. Clay
Rick Iasiello
Marion Pont
George Hayes
Erling Christensen
Leslie Manchester
Manuel Maderia
Samuel Roderick
Morris Thompson
Mark Middleton
Arthur H. Banks
Eugene Willett
Benjamin L. Tuthill
Joseph Roderick Jr.

Fishermen's Monument at Town Dock.